A
DANGEROUS
COMBINATION

SANDY DEROUIN
STEPHANIE DIROCCO

A DANGEROUS COMBINATION

Living with a Bipolar Alcoholic

TATE PUBLISHING & Enterprises

Published by Tate Publishing & Enterprises, LLC
127 E. Trade Center Terrace | Mustang, Oklahoma 73064 USA
1.888.361.9473 | www.tatepublishing.com

Tate Publishing is committed to excellence in the publishing industry. The company reflects the philosophy established by the founders, based on Psalm 68:11,
"The Lord gave the word and great was the company of those who published it."

Book design copyright © 2011 by Tate Publishing, LLC. All rights reserved.
Cover design by Amber Gulilat
Interior design by Lindsay B. Behrens

Published in the United States of America

ISBN: 978-1-61777-329-7
Biography & Autobiography / Personal Memoirs/Alcoholism
11.03.21

We dedicate this book to our dad, who always enjoyed life
and lived each day to the fullest. We miss you!

ACKNOWLEDGEMENTS

This book would not have been possible without the support from my family and friends. Their patience and understanding was necessary as I spent long hours attempting to recollect so many moments of my life. I needed their ears to listen as I spoke of my ideas, and I utilized their useful suggestions. At times, I may have been short tempered and overwhelmed, but I always felt their unconditional love.

My gratitude must be expressed to the wonderful artists whose music and inspirational lyrics comforted me. Often, I felt like they were singing directly to me. My favorite radio station 104.7 the Fish has captured my heart and given me so many hours of listening pleasure. When the voices in my head were too much to handle, I was able to replace them with beautiful melodies that inspired my soul and helped to erase any negative feelings.

To the support offered from those at Alanon, I offer my sincerest thanks. In times of despair, it is nice to know that there are people who share your concerns and are ready to offer knowledgeable advice. Unfamiliar with alcoholism, I was unprepared to handle the adversity this brought to my life and desperately needed the support from experts and others who shared my misery. While my responses were not always 100 percent correct, their teachings were always in the back of my mind, and many of my decisions came from their recommendations.

I must never forget the one main source of my strength and where it came from. Without the support from God and his undying love, I never could have survived. In my most sorrowful moments, I would look up to the heavens and beg him to lead me. I heard his whispers and they did lead me in the right direction. Thank you, Lord.

INTRODUCTION

I have grown to appreciate my humble beginnings, and I am thankful for the simple pleasures God has given me. I felt compelled to share my life with others because I hope my story gives inspiration and hope too many.

A book was the perfect opportunity to reach others yet still remain private. I never wanted to force my husband or family into the spotlight, but I felt an overwhelming need to shed light on the afflictions my husband suffered from. All too common, these diseases affect many and often go undiagnosed. I have learned not to blame or judge but rather listen and support with a patient and open heart. I hope the pages of my book give others in similar situations the desire to read and find comfort in knowing that they are not alone.

Throughout this long and often painful journey, I sought the support and unconditional love of family, friends, and most importantly the Lord. Sharing my dream with my sister, I was able to organize the pieces of my life, and together we wrote this book as a healing process for our family and to serve as a model for others.

Hopefully the fulfillment of my dream will influence others to seek theirs.

At first, the notion of writing a book was something I could not fathom. I sought the help from my parish priest. He offered me his blessing as well as encouragement. No, this would not be easy, but with God's strength I would overcome the challenges of this task. If I followed in God's footsteps, I was certain he would guide me in the right direction.

I now better understand why God chose this journey for me. While we may disagree with our chosen path, there is light at the end of every tunnel. If I had chosen a different route, I might not be sharing this story today, nor would I be able to encourage others. There were many times throughout my life that I wanted to give up, turn back, or veer off track. However, my faith kept me strong. Facing adversity, I have become a much stronger person. You must always believe in yourself, follow your heart, and make the choices that you feel are right and can live with. Today and always, I am willing to place my trust in the Lord.

1

My parents, John and Ann, were married on November 11, 1958. Soon after, they began living the American dream. They purchased a small starter home in Warwick, Rhode Island. Nine months later, they were blessed with a healthy baby. They called their first daughter Suzanne. Sharon came quickly, only ten and one half months later. Abiding by the Catholic method of birth control would prove quite eventful. Because of a medical condition, Ann had to undergo an operation, leaving her with just a half of an ovary. Even still she was able to conceive. Ann gave birth to me on December 17, 1962. I was named Sandy, keeping with the *S* tradition. My parents were surprised when they discovered that my mother was pregnant once again. The doctor was sure that this baby was a boy. Thankful to have a boy to finish off their family, Steven would be a welcome addition. However, Steven soon became Stephanie. Stephanie did not disappoint my sports-loving father. She was the son they never had and participated in many sports. Within six short but active years, my family had been formed. With four girls to support, my parents would certainly face financial challenges. However, my father had a steady job as a probation officer, and my mother helped out by conducting door-to-door surveys. Our lives were not extravagant, but I always felt secure in our small modest home.

In the sixties, our family's income would be considered middle class. Although my mother had four girls to dress, she improvised by sewing coats and dresses often in color-coordinated fabrics. We have many pictures of me and my three sisters decked out in our Sunday best. On Sunday, we would go to the Catholic Church as a family to participate in Mass. My mother would often suffer panic attacks in church and have to leave abruptly. Eventually the stress of raising a family took a toll on my mother's body. She suffered a nervous breakdown and had to stay in bed for a while. I was young when this happened and do not have clear memories of my mother's breakdown. It is just as well. These are images that are sad to remember, but are necessary to recall. I have learned that life's burdens can affect your health physically, as well as emotionally.

At the age of five, I moved from the city of Warwick to the town of West Warwick. My recollection of living in a small state had warped my perception. I thought that all states had small cities and towns in close proximity. Boy, would my views change in the future.

As a child, I have wonderful memories of growing up in a close knit Italian family. My father's French-Canadian heritage took a backseat to our Italian traditions. Being that my father was an only child, we visited mostly with my mother's side of the family. After Mass, my family would travel to Providence to visit with our relatives. My mother was the oldest of three children. I adored my aunt and uncle. My aunt was often compared to Sally Field. She was so beautiful and sweet. We would all meet at my memere and papa's bungalow. Although the house was small, we all were able to gather and enjoy a family meal. To make room for everyone, my grandparents had an additional table set up in a spare bedroom. We ate as a family, not in front of the television as many families do today. The smells of home cooking would linger throughout the house. I can still see my memere (an Italian grandmother with a French name) in the pantry, stirring a huge pot of spaghetti sauce. After dinner, my papa would take the grandchildren for a Sunday drive. To some, my papa would appear gruff. However, he loved his grandchildren and often displayed his affection. In the evening, we would gather in the living room to watch the Lawrence Welk show. My papa would sit in *his* chair and smoke paroles. Sadly, he died of colon cancer at the young age of sixty. I was only ten years old. Even though I may have been young, I still remember the sadness I felt and how much I missed him. Unfortunately, medical screening was not as efficient in the sixties as it is today.

During the summer, my family would meet at Goddard Park after church. My memere's spaghetti sauce was not left behind. We would simmer the sauce over the grills and enjoy macaroni for lunch. Our day was filled with games of croquette, cards, and horse-shoes. We would stay into the evening and feast on hamburger and hotdogs for dinner. For dessert, my parents would always pick up Dunkin' Donuts. Today, this donut shop exists on almost every street corner in Rhode Island. I recall my humble Uncle Joe's words, "I wonder what all the poor people are doing." We may not have been rich, but our memories were. I wish I could have created simi-lar memories for my children

When I was in elementary school, I began going to catechism after school. My friends and I would walk down the street to another building for class. I remember the nuns and unfortunately, I also remember wanting the hour to end. I was anxious to rush home so I could watch my favorite show, *Dark Shadows*. Television did not dictate my life. With only a couple of stations to watch (cable did not exist), enjoyment came from being outdoors. We played simple games, not video games. We played with friends, not by ourselves. We were not afraid of being outdoors and riding our bikes. We did not worry about being kidnapped. Unfortunately, children today are not so lucky, and parents are rightfully concerned. Ironically, I do not think we even locked our doors. Today, we keep them alarmed. Parents did not need to block the shows that their children watched. *Bewitched, I Dream of Jeanie,* and *Gilligan's Island* were a few of my favorites. Today, the shows are not geared for family viewing, and we need to monitor what our children are watching and how they may be influenced.

My youth was filled with so many great memories. Visiting my aunt at her home in Providence was the best. The tantalizing smell of fish and chips permeated her apartment and made my mouth water. She lived in an apartment, which hovered over a fish and chip restaurant. On Fridays, my mother would treat us to a dinner of fish and chips.

On Christmas Eve, my family would celebrate at our home. The food and presents were abundant, and our spirits were grateful. I fondly remember one Christmas Eve in particular. The skies were filled with snow, and as I gazed upward, I swore I caught a glimpse of Santa on his sleigh. I quickly ran upstairs and was amazed to see that indeed Santa had arrived. Presents for my sisters and I were spewed under our tree. Years later, I would learn that my father's mother (my French grandmother) would help pay for some of our presents. My dear generous memere was an integral part of our family. She was a snowbird. She lived in Florida during the winter and came home to Rhode Island in the summer. My father had lost his dad when he was only twenty years old. My grandfather was twenty years older than my grandmother. Thankfully, we still had his mother to love and cherish.

Time seemed to tick slowly by then. Today, I realize that it passes much too quickly. For three years, my father worked on building our future home. Once again, we moved one town over. To save money, my father labored and built our house himself. I was amazed at his accomplishment. Thinking back, I wish my parents were able and willing to let us join extra-curricular activities. I would not say that they denied us these opportunities; however, I can say that we were not encouraged. God knows, children need to be pushed. My parents were determined to save twenty cents for every dollar that they earned. This has led to a comfortable nest egg in their retirement. I suppose being frugal can pay off, and I could learn from this.

I was able to finish off the fourth grade in my old school. My father would drive my younger sister and me to school each day so that our transition into our new school would take place the following year. As we drove, the song "Red Hot Lincoln" would play from the radio. It's funny how we associate experiences and music. This song triggered content and happy memories. Fortunately, my new home was only ten minutes from my old house. I was able to stay in touch with friends for a while. Thankfully, we did not move out of state.

Beginning fifth grade in a new school went smoothly. My forward and outgoing nature was a quality that allowed me to quickly make new friends. However, many of these friends were boys, and my attraction to them at eleven deemed more than friendship. I guess you could say I was boy crazy. Today, I wish my parents were more aware of this, because I believe that my youth was focused too much on relationships and less on academics. My mother had decided to return to college and pursue a degree in nursing.

While this was a great opportunity for her, I believe it had some negative impact on my childhood. My parents did not pay much attention to my lack of studies; therefore, I continued to just get by in school, giving little effort or quite simply "just enough." My days were filled completing chores, babysitting, and steady boyfriends. In the seventies, the going rate for an hour of babysitting was a dollar. Today, this amount may appear ridiculous, but it was relative to the times. A hamburger at McDonalds was a mere twenty-five cents. I would not allow my fourteen year old daughter to date. Most importantly, I wonder why my parents allowed me to get in a boy's car at such a young age. The seventies were sure different. As a parent, I would not be quite so naïve. My experiences have made me more aware and involved.

A DANGEROUS COMBINATION

During this time, I became acquainted with two sisters who were twins. My new best friends seemed to have everything. From ski boats to a winter home in New Hampshire, their lives were filled with material objects, objects my family could not afford. They were rich, pretty, and athletic. I was so lucky to have them as friends, or so I thought. Being in the cool crowd had some pretty wonderful perks. My summers were a blast, as I attempted to learn how to water ski. My athleticism was not quite up to par. While the twins could scale great jumps on their skis, I was afraid of heights. Looking back, I now realize that I was growing up way too quickly. Being cool also meant smoking cigarettes, courting boys, and social-izing in school. School was not geared for learning. My grades in school reflected my lack of effort. Settling for As, Bs, and Cs, I was content with average grades. For me, my future educational endeav-ors would be the Community College Rhode Island (CCRI), not a university. Unlike my older sister, I did not want to be a nurse, and a four-year degree seemed insignificant. Today, I regret this decision. Perhaps if my parents demanded more I would have given more, but we cannot undo what has been done and can only go forward.

When my snowbird grandmother was home for the summer, she lived upstairs from our home in an in-law apartment. We were so lucky to have her living so close. Every Saturday evening at promptly 4:40, my grandmother would leave for church. She needed to arrive early for the five o'clock Mass to guarantee her usual seat. There she would sit, third row up from the back of the church, always at the end of the pew. I can still hear her singing her favorite hymn, "Let There Be Peace on Earth." As a teenager, I could not fathom how she could love church so much. As an adult, I can fully understand her passion. Oh, how I wish I could talk to her today. I have so many questions I would like to ask her and so much I would love to share. Perhaps when we meet in heaven, I can resolve these issues. My grandmother was taken from us so quickly and unexpectedly while in Florida. She died peacefully in her sleep the day after Christmas. This seemed an appropriate way to die for such a kind and gentle woman. Oh, how I wished I could have spoken to her one last time. Sometimes, we wait too long to tell others that we love and admire them.

I was sitting in Algebra II in the tenth grade when I heard a boy with a southern drawl speaking. Nobody in my class could understand him, but I found him quite interesting. I knew that he must be from the South, even though we had not been formally introduced. Time passed, and I continued dating numerous boys. I would become bored in a relationship, and my eyes would begin to stray. I never became too serious with any boy. Ironically, this would change when the blond, southern teen who sat three seats in front of me in Algebra II crossed my path outside of school, accidentally. My younger sister, Stephanie, was asked to babysit for a family after school. She had to decline because she would not be out of school in time. Instead, I was offered and gladly accepted the job. Little did I know, this southern cutie from my Algebra II class lived right next door. I think I already had a boyfriend at the time; however, as I mentioned before, my eyes were always wandering. I now had my goals set on Frank. I asked a friend who was acquainted with him to mention me and my interest for him. She called me back and said Frank was indeed interested in going out with me. I quickly accepted his offer, unaware that he was listening on the other end of the phone. This was the beginning of what would become a long-term relationship for Frank and me.

The relationship I established with Frank did not tone down my wily ways. I still continued looking at other boys and spent most nights out partying with friends. My eleventh grade year was quite eventful, and it was not academic. I was either out dating, babysitting, or frequenting nightclubs. At the time, the legal drinking age was eighteen. However, I was still able to get into most clubs with a fake ID. My best friends were still the twins. In my senior year, I did not attend the senior prom, because most of my friends, including the twins, were a year ahead of me. Growing up in high school, I acted out well beyond my young years. I'm surprised my parents did not catch on and stop my behavior. Unfortunately, they didn't, and I grew up way too quickly and experienced too much too soon. I now realize you cannot go back and relive your high school years. I will never have another senior prom.

One of the most pleasant and loving memories I had in my youth was the adoration I felt for my pets. My mother was not what you would consider an animal lover. In fact, she didn't really like animals. She broke down and bought us the most adorable puppy named Fluffy. I loved him so much. I was also allowed to have a hamster that I named Butterball. Sadly, Butterball did not live very long. My mother made me house him in the basement. I think he may have died because it was too cold without the heat during the winter. I do not blame my mother, but I do question her decision. I grew up and loved all animals, including my fish. My pets are truly an extension of my family and are always nearby.

In 1980, I graduated high school and began taking courses at CCRI for computer science. During this time, I was waitressing at a local restaurant. My life was busy with school, work, and Frank. One evening I had made plans to go out with Frank. To my dismay, I was also on call at the restaurant. The manager called and said my help was needed. I did not want to break my date and told the manager that I was unable to fill in. She told me not to return. Fortunately, I was able to quickly find other employment at a retail store. Back in the eighties, the unemployment rate did not affect my opportunities. At this time, Frank was also pursuing his education at CCRI. His parents had moved back south, leaving Frank up north with me. Then his father called with a request that would change our lives. He wanted Frank to move south to join the company he had established. Frank was being pulled in two directions. The opportunity that his father provided was quite tempting, yet he did not want to leave me. He would go, but he insisted that I leave with him. I had just begun college yet was easily persuaded to quit. At the young age of seventeen, I was making a very grown-up decision. My Catholic religion and Frank's Methodist upbringing influenced our decision to get married. Living together was not acceptable by either of our families. My sister Sharon had also married at the young age of eighteen. Her marriage only lasted a year, but that didn't mean mine would end in divorce. I was hopeful that my love for Frank would endure. On January 24, 1981, Frank and I were married in a simple ceremony. I had visions of an easy marriage with all the aspirations that woman long for. I dreamed of a house with a white picket fence, a loving husband returning from a long day at work, and babies there to happily greet him. I never imagined my life would take another route.

2

To think, I had not even met my future in-laws. Here I was marrying a man whose family I had never met, moving a thousand miles away from home, and not even thinking about the consequences. I would miss family birthdays, holidays, and the births of nieces and nephews. Being so young and naïve, I did not even know how to plan a wedding. I was one of my sister Sharon's bridesmaids, but I had not helped in the preparations. I accomplished the easy tasks by purchasing a dress for two hundred dollars and a diamond ring for three hundred. Frank agreed to marry in the Catholic Church, even though he had been raised Methodist. We had to convince the church to let us forgo the six month preparation and classes we should have participated in. They obliged and together, our vows sealed the marriage. Ironically, the words spoken in a Catholic ceremony by both partners would grow to have significant meaning for me in the future. When I said, "I take thee for better or worse," the impact would be felt for years to come.

The bridal shower and reception were quite simple. I had one of the twins as my maid of honor. I did not have a trail of bridesmaids, nor a cute flower girl and ring bearer. Most brides plan their wedding for at least one year; I only had a few months. I could not believe that I was not only gaining a new family, I would also be losing my own. Surprisingly, my parents did not try to stop me. I could not believe that they were oblivious to the fact that their daughter was moving one thousand miles away to Atlanta, Georgia. Regardless of how they felt, they did not let on. Thankfully, my in-laws seemed really sweet. So on a cold, snowy January day, Frank and I were married. While many newlyweds spent their first evenings on a tropical island enjoying their honeymoon, I spent my first evening in a nasty hotel room. The next day, we watched the Super Bowl with a few friends. This was not my idea of romance! Our honeymoon began the next day as we drove to our new home in Georgia.

En route to Georgia, Frank and I stopped in New York, Washington, and Virginia. I was able to meet his relatives. Most brides get to meet their extended family at their wedding. However, I only invited the immediate family and missed out on a big lavish affair. My journey to Georgia only lasted about one week. It was almost surreal to think that this journey would actually last for most of my adult years. When I said goodbye to my family, I didn't realize what this goodbye would mean. I was only thinking about two months ahead. I did not even consider that I may have been too young and naïve to get married. Regardless of my skepticism now, I recognize that this was my faith and the path chosen for me.

Once I arrived in Georgia, I realized that Rhode Island was much different. I enjoyed the warm weather that Georgia offered and would not miss the brutal winters. Also Frank's family was much different than mine. They were quiet and reserved. I thought all families were loud. Frank has two younger brothers. Bill was my age, and Steve was two years younger than me. I was able to savor delicious home cooked meals prepared by Jeanette, Frank's mother. Seeing that I was a novice in the kitchen, it was a relief to have Jeanette as a mother-in-law. We lived with my in-laws for the first four months to save some money and transition into our new lives and careers. Frank started working with his father, Frank Sr., in sales, and I began working at a retail store called Richway. After being a sales clerk for a while, they asked me to work in the cash office. I counted money all day long, and believe me, this got old really quick.

I decided to change employment and sought the help of a service called Kelly Girl. My secretarial skills were put to the test. Even though my performance was substandard, I secured a job in downtown Atlanta in account receivables. In 1982, computers were not the rage like today. I learned the basic skills and earned four dollars and ten cents an hour for my services. I enjoyed the people I worked with. Together, I would smoke cigarettes with my colleagues, surprisingly right within our office. Thankfully, for the health of so many, this has been outlawed today. I was disappointed to learn that I would not be receiving a raise after over a year of employment. Unfortunately, my boss's partner was stealing from the company. My boss was not privy to the theft, because he was too consumed with the bottle. This was my first experience with alcoholism. While my husband and I were keen to partying, I did not associate this behavior as a problem or a disease. People around me were drinking, yet I paid it little mind. Thus far, alcohol was not negatively impacting my life, or so I thought. After a year and a half, I decided to look for a new job, knowing that I was not climbing the financial ladder where I was.

Frank and I had already become financially independent and were living in an apartment of our own. We had found a one bedroom apartment that cost $315.00 a month, including utilities. We had a blast furnishing our home with modest purchases. Cooking dinner was a new and exciting experience that I relished. Even though it was only canned vegetables and fried pork chops, dinner was prepared by me. I was quickly adjusting to being a wife at the young age of eighteen. Frank was also transitioning to his job well. He soon began traveling with his dad, successfully selling cup dispensers. Frank introduced me to a few of his high school friends. Along with people I befriended at work and acquaintances from our new apartment, I enjoyed hanging by the pool, soaking in the southern sun.

Every year in June, Frank's family would vacation in North Myrtle Beach, South Carolina. As a family tradition, cousins from Wisconsin and Virginia would reunite with those from Georgia and enjoy the beautiful waters and fun atmosphere that Myrtle Beach offered. My in-laws would stay for an entire month. Frank and I went for one week and spent most of this time mingling with his extended family. We rocked out to bands such as Styx, Blondie, and Devo. Carefree and lighthearted, I enjoyed myself immensely. Frank's family had a pop-up trailer, and we slept in a tent outside. We vacationed simply, yet I fondly remember those years. The following year, my parents and younger sister would come too, and soon they would begin their own yearly tradition. For me, Myrtle Beach represented a place where our families would gather and rehash the year's events. Soon, grandchildren and pets would join our clan.

Frank and I decided to add to our family. Since we were still living in the apartment, we settled on a parrot that we named Burt. We quickly became attached to our new pet. Then one afternoon, in our apartment, we heard someone screaming "Fire!" Frank and I immediately grabbed what we could and ran outside. We did not leave our loving bird behind. However, Burt was not used to being in his cage and was quite agitated. Foolishly, we decided to let him out of his cage. To our surprise, sirens began going off. Scared, Burt flew from my hand. He disappeared into the trees. I was devastated! Hopeful that he would return, I left his cage filled with food in the woods. For days, I helplessly called his name, but to no avail. Burt did not return home. To lessen our loss, Frank and I stupidly replaced Burt with a skunk. We bought him because we were assured that he was de-scented and could not spray. Soon after he joined our family, we had to travel to Rhode Island for my sister Suzanne's wedding. Even though he could not damage a room with his scent, Coco tore apart my parent's basement carpet with his claws. Needless to say, they were not very happy. My sister and her husband had both graduated from college and were getting married after planning their wedding for one year. I guess this is how she expected couples to plan their future, because her comments to Frank and I displayed her displeasure for our quick wedding.

She doubted Frank's business abilities because he lacked a formal education. This upset my husband, and he became determined to prove her wrong. Putting our negative feelings aside, we enjoyed her beautiful wedding. My sister Sharon had to travel from Florida where she lived to attend the wedding. As fate often intervenes, Sharon's future would also change from this visit. While in Rhode Island, she went to a night club for dancing and drinks. Unknown to her, Sharon met her future husband that night. She returned to Florida for a short time but chose to come back to Rhode Island to marry the man she encountered that fateful evening. I also left Rhode Island after the wedding, but my new home was waiting for me in Georgia.

Back in Georgia, Coco began showing signs of animosity toward my husband. We decided that it would be best to give him up for adoption. Sadly, I had to say good-bye to another pet, but I knew it was for the best. Even though we were still in the apartment and space was limited, our next choice for a pet was more typical. We decided on man's best friend. Caesar, a Doberman pinscher, entered our lives. Cute yet feisty, Caesar behaved like most puppies do and did his share of damage to our apartment and furnishings. Meanwhile, Frank and his father's company was becoming financially lucrative. Happily, Frank and I began looking for our first home. Still having fun partying, we were bringing some stability to our lives by choosing to wisely invest in a house. Thinking back now, I guess some of our decisions were mature and responsible. This was surely a good beginning.

We were fortunate to find a home for about $80,000 in a neighborhood close to Frank's office. Moving into our new house was pretty terrific. The facade was conservative, much like me. I did not wear fancy clothes and looked much like the girl next door. My home was a typical split-level, but Frank and I were able to buy it new and decide on the final touches. Even though I may not have appreciated our good fortunes then, I now realize how blessed we were. Some families are not fortunate enough to ever own their homes. In our early twenties, Frank and I were living the American dream.

Close to our new home, our new "best friends" resided on twenty acres of land. We met this couple who lived nearby and quickly forged a relationship. Wow, were they rich! I felt like I was a kid again hanging out with the twins. We spent a lot of time together with our new friends, enjoying their horses and vast house. Frank enjoyed making fried chicken wings, and I loved concocting my grandmother's infamous spaghetti sauce. We would often invite friends over to our home to share some home cooking. During these visits Frank and I, along with our guests, would enjoy some cocktails. Perhaps too many drinks were consumed. At this time, I was unaware how serious drinking would become in my life and affect my family. Unfortunately, my immature and naïve mentality did not put a stop to it then.

One year after our traditional visit to Myrtle Beach, my younger sister and Frank's cousin from Wisconsin decided to come to Georgia and extend their vacation. One unforgettable night, we decided to go to a Georgia nightclub. It was a Wednesday evening and the place was quite empty. An employee approached my sister and me and asked if we were interested in participating in a bikini contest. Hesitant at first, we declined. However, after several minutes and relentless begging by the employee, we finally gave in. As we were changing into our borrowed swimsuits, we observed the other contestants primping in the mirrors and rubbing oil all over their tanned bodies. My sister and I began questioning our decision but decided to go ahead. Why not? There were only a few spectators, or so we thought. When we stepped on stage, the crowd roared. Suddenly, all these men appeared. Embarrassed, my sister and I wanted to run off the stage. Needless to say, neither one of us won. We laugh about this incident today and mock our stupidity. I do not believe that either one of us would have taken part in this if alcohol was not present at the nightclub that evening. Our better judgment was skewed.

We visited Rhode Island again after my sister Susan gave birth to her first baby. She was gorgeous, just perfect. I could not envision myself pregnant. Frank and I had not yet contemplated beginning a family. Perhaps someday it would happen, but not just yet.

I was now settling into a new job at Allstate Insurance as a secretary. Frank's office was right next door. How convenient. Constantly, I was still being asked, "Where are you from?" I guess my northern accent was still very apparent. As time passed, I was sure people would accept me as a southerner. Ironically, I am still asked this question. I may have given up my northern roots, but some traits will linger forever. Overall, I am happy with my decision and realize there are certain things I must get used to. Sometimes feeling like an outsider and life without my blood relatives are two such examples.

Fights would sometimes break out between Frank and me. Growing up, I often witnessed shouting matches between my parents. For me, our behavior seemed fairly normal. Thinking back, I can trace the time these bouts broke out. Most often, it was after we had been drinking. At the time, this seemed okay because I did not believe either Frank or I had an issue with alcohol. We both were productive in the workplace and able to pay all of our bills. I was loving my life, my job, and my marriage to Frank. Sure we had our share of fights. Who doesn't?

We took another trip to New England to see my new nephew. My sister Susan had another baby to complete her family. He was so perfect! I'm grateful that Frank and I were able to continue our visits, and I did not miss out on these milestones. During this trip, my father inquired about Frank's and my chances of also starting a family. Perhaps after four years of marriage, our time was now. I became pregnant after only two months of trying. There are couples who try for years. Fortunate yet weary, I did not know what to expect, so I purchased a book about the changes that occur from month to month in regard to the fetus. I also had to make a couple of changes. All I could think about was delivering a healthy baby. Therefore, I immediately quit smoking and put an end to partying, for now.

Our family also had grown with the addition of a new parrot. Intimidating at first, Sam soon became a friend to Frank and me. He would have to. It is common for an African Grey to live to be at least sixty. He could very well outlive us. Soon this amazing and intelligent bird began mimicking us and talking on cue. Sam would be with us for a very long time.

Frank's company was becoming quite successful. If this continued, I assumed I would be quitting my job when the baby arrived. Frank's brothers had also gotten married, and his younger brother's wife would take over my job at Allstate. I became very fond of my sisters-in-laws. They filled a void in my life since I had to leave my own sisters behind.

Financially, our lives were on an upswing. We decided to look for a new home in a safer neighborhood before the baby arrived. We found a beautiful brick front Georgian traditional. It had four bedrooms and two and one half baths. There was plenty of room to expand our family. Most importantly, the backyard was big and somewhat level. Perhaps my dream of owning a pool would come true. I had admired my friend's pool. I enjoyed picking out the wallpaper and paint colors to decorate my home. I still felt like a novice and sought the advice of the builder's wife. She loved country, and I believed I did too. Come to find out, my taste was actually traditional. Oh well, I would have to live with a country kitchen for a while. Things could certainly be worse. Moving into our new home on Easter weekend could seem overwhelming, but I was overjoyed because I had a new baby coming, a beautiful home, and a successful husband. I was so lucky.

We still kept in touch with our old neighbors. One evening, Frank and I were invited to go to his friend's thirtieth birthday party at his brother-in-law's house. Pregnant and miserable, I could not tolerate the heavy drinking that was going on. Things looked differently from this bird's eye view. I watched as Frank consumed an awful lot of alcohol. Some would think that this was a wake-up call for me but it wasn't, not yet. I became extremely upset when Frank, the birthday boy, and others were flashed by a couple of female guests. I wanted to leave immediately, but Frank refused. I was being labeled a nag by my husband while these promiscuous women were shown admiration. This was ridiculous! I became privy to a new side of my husband's character, and I did not like it. I did not speak a word to him on the drive home, nor did I sleep with him in bed. I would never hurt him the way he hurt me, and I felt he deserved my cold shoulder for a while.

I had decided I wanted to deliver my baby naturally. Frank and I joined a Lamaze class to prepare ourselves. I discovered that having a baby naturally was difficult and not having my family nearby was also painful. They were not here to share in my joy. To ease my sorrow, I had found my way back to church. Deep down, I knew this was a place I would go every Sunday for years to come. Since Frank was not Catholic, I accepted the fact that I would be going alone. The seeds to my faith had been planted and would soon begin to flourish.

3

The baby's room was ready, and so was I. June was approaching, and we were only a few weeks away from my due date. Frank's family and I were very anxious. This would be their first grandchild. Unfortunately, we would be missing our yearly trip to Myrtle Beach. Fortunately, my water broke on my exact due date. The waiting was finally over. We arrived at the hospital at 8:00 a.m., and soon thereafter, the contractions began. Doing this naturally, I was not given any medication to ease the excruciating pain. By one o'clock, I was fully dilated. This could not come soon enough. The pain was unbearable. My baby's head was so large that the doctor had to cut an incision to allow for passage. Using forceps, the doctor began releasing the baby from my womb. They discovered that the umbilical cord was wrapped around the baby's neck. With God's grace, Maryanne overcame this setback and entered the world weighing eight pounds, four ounces, and measuring twenty-one and three-quarter inches. She was the prettiest baby I had ever seen. I stayed in the hospital for a few days and bonded with my new daughter. Back in the eighties, healthcare providers allowed for this extra time. Today, women are not awarded this luxury. I chose to breast-feed Maryanne. It was convenient compared to making bottles and worrying about the temperature of the formula. Also I will always cherish the closeness I felt during this time to my daughter and value the importance I felt for her well-being.

Maryanne was a great baby. I enjoyed being a new mom and easily adjusted into this role. When Maryanne was six weeks old, my parents came to meet their new grandchild. I was so happy to have them but became melancholy when they had to leave. I hated the idea that they would be deaf to her first words and not witness her first steps. I was also disappointed that my sisters had not yet met their new niece. On a happier note, Maryanne would soon be baptized, and the ceremony was in Rhode Island. Thankfully, my relatives would get to share this blessed moment with my daughter and us. My in-laws would also be traveling to Rhode Island to be part of this celebration.

Business continued to grow for Frank's company. His brothers, Bill and Steve, had also joined the ranks. Often, I would remind Frank that he was very lucky to see his family every day. I may have been guilty of repeating myself, but I was always conscious of the sacrifices I had made. I loved living in the South and was thankful for the opportunities offered to my family, yet it was difficult giving up so much of my past. I did look forward to the trips we took to Rhode Island and was hopeful that our financial future will allow us to continue our visits.

By the spring of the following year, I began to worry about Caesar, our Doberman pinscher. He was so large, and I felt threatened for the sake of my baby. I was forced to keep him in the garage because our backyard was not fenced. I knew this was not a proper existence for the dog and believed he would be better off with a new environment. While I was in Rhode Island for a visit, Frank received a call from a family that was interested in adopting Caesar. They had a huge farm and plenty of room for him to roam. Frank met them nearby, and Caesar got into their car. When I returned to

Georgia, Caesar was gone. I never had the chance to say good-bye. Sadly, I knew this was the right decision, but I wish Frank could have waited. He had not asked for their telephone number; therefore, I could not call to check on him and was denied the opportunity to occasionally visit.

My desires for a pool heightened. The refreshing cool waters would provide some relief from the humid summers of Georgia. Installing an underground pool was not a simple task. Septic lines ran throughout our backyard. Workers had to reposition the lines to the front yard. This was an added expense that we initially had not planned for. At twenty-five, I took an awful lot for granted. I failed to realize how fortunate I was to have a pool, and best of all, I could spend time enjoying it with my beautiful daughter. Lucky to be a stay-at-home mom, I shared many days relaxing by the pool with my baby and friends.

Continuing our partying ways, Frank and I often met up with old friends and began meeting new ones. Our neighbor from around the corner invited us to a semiformal Christmas party. Unfamiliar with this type of festivity, I ended up having a great time. During this time, I began to scrutinize Frank's social habits. He seemed to enjoy drinking a little too much. With a baby to care for, I chose to act responsibly and tried not to lose control. However, Frank did not share my inhibitions. His career in sales required frequent trips and time away from home. He was not under my watchful eye, nor was he concerned with the daily care of a baby. His job became second nature. For most of my married life, he was traveling, and I had accepted this. Perhaps I was being too sensitive to his so-called overindulgence. As they often say, if you work hard you deserve to play hard. I shared the same dilemma with my sister-in-law Lynn. Recently, she and my brother-in-law Steve had their first baby. Like Frank, Steve had to travel often. Lynn often sought my advice. She found this lifestyle hard to swallow and did not like the burden of raising a baby all on her shoulders. Comparing our duties, I consoled Lynn and told her she was lucky to have Steve as a husband. I envied the help Steve provided when he was at home. Frank was not so helpful.

Frank began working on finishing a room in the basement. He wished for a bar room where he could play pool with friends. His desires seemed innocent. One of Frank's finishing touches was a neon sign that glowed, "Kick back at Frank's." Unfortunately, this room led to misery. Soon our lives began centering on drinking. From Myrtle Beach to our daily lives, a day would not go by without Frank having a cocktail. We began to fight constantly, and our dissention came from Frank's apparent abuse. However, this was recognized by me, and not yet discovered by Frank.

We decided to adopt a new four-month-old puppy. This time we decided on a show quality Shar-Pei. Hopefully, we could mate our dog with an exceptional male, and she could mother some puppies of the same degree. I was relieved to have a backyard that was fenced in. Now my dog could play freely and be outside with us when we were enjoying the pool. I knew in my heart that I could never give up another pet and was determined never to feel this type of regret again.

My life was going along fairly smoothly until I received some devastating news. My dear aunt had passed away at the young age of forty from breast cancer. She had battled this terminal disease for five years, until succumbing to its effects in June. I had just seen her in May when I traveled to Rhode Island for my sister Stephanie's wedding. She appeared so courageous and danced all evening, even though I knew she was weak. My aunt had opted out of taking the traditional chemo and radiation methods of treating cancer. I often wonder if she would be alive today if she had followed this regimen. I had to go back North in June to attend her funeral. Leaving behind two young children ages ten and thirteen, my aunt left this earth too soon. To this day, my family has never gotten over this loss. The only consolation I feel is when I think of my deserving aunt spending eternity in heaven. Every year, my uncle places a remembrance in the paper for her. His writing is so eloquent and true to my aunt's character.

My oldest sister and her family came for a visit and fell in love with Georgia. They decided to sell their home in Massachusetts and relocate one half-mile from my house. I couldn't believe it. Finally, I could share my life with family. My sister was a nurse and worked the evening shift. She needed me to babysit my three-year-old nephew daily. Even though it was an adjustment, I was thankful that Maryanne had a cousin to play with. It was a blessing to watch my sister's kids grow up. Ironically, I would also need my sister's shoulder in the future when my life began spiraling out of control.

Our dog was going through another heat. We knew it was a good time to try to mate her. Our attempt was successful, and she became pregnant. We intended to sell the puppies but deep down, I knew I would become immediately attached. Without any complications, two healthy puppies were born in our master bedroom. What an amazing experience! However, these tiny creatures are a lot of work. In a short time, they began sprouting hair and the wrinkles characteristic of this breed began to form. Eight weeks sped by, and we knew a decision had to be made. As I first thought giving these puppies up for adoption would be difficult. Ultimately, we placed an ad in the paper, hoping for a prospective buyer. I mentioned that we were looking for a buyer and not two buyers. As you might have inferred, we decided to keep one of the puppies. Our house was becoming full. We now had two dogs and a parrot to care for. Frankly, *I* had two dogs and a parrot to care for because most of the caretaking was done by me.

Now that Maryanne was a toddler, I thought we should try for another baby. However, this experience was quite different than the first. Sex was extremely painful, and I began to worry. Baffled, my doctor began running numerous tests to try to put a name on my discomfort. He concluded that I had trichomonas. Clueless,

A DANGEROUS COMBINATION

I did what I was told, and Frank and I took our prescribed pills. Embarrassed, I had my neighbor pick them up for me because he was our local pharmacist. Much later, I became educated about this infection and discovered that it was an STD. My doctor had not informed me of this. Perhaps he was trying to protect me, but I wished I had known. If I had suspected my husband, I would have never continued on my quest to have another baby. Once again, I was being naïve.

Frank was traveling on business a lot and continuing to drink just as much. He had quite an ego and could have used a large slice of humble pie. My sister-in-law Wendy decided to file for divorce from my brother-in-law Bill. Like Frank, he did not put much effort into his marriage. Unlike me, Wendy did something about it. She moved to Chicago and went back to school. Of course I felt bad for Bill, but I also could see Wendy's perspective. However, Frank the manipulator forbid me to talk to her and completely blamed her for the breakup. How typical!

Frank's company was planning their yearly convention that took place every fall. This year, the convention was being held in California. Spouses were encouraged to attend this trip. Seeing as I had never been to California, I gladly accepted the invitation. My relationship with Frank seemed to be fairly amicable; besides, I was still unaware that he had contracted an STD and passed it along to me. Frank bestowed a concrete gift to me right before we left. Parked in my driveway was a new Mitsubishi Eclipse, complete with a big red bow. How thoughtful and generous. Leaving for California, I felt pretty content. Unfortunately, we had to leave Maryanne home with my in-laws and sister. Confident that she was in loving hands, I was hopeful that Frank and I would bond on this trip and spend quality time together. Perhaps things were looking up after all.

Upon arriving in San Francisco in the fall of 1989, we experienced a few tremors. The city had just experienced an earthquake, but we were not frightened off and still continued our trip. We did not witness the devastation that affected some areas, but we did see some buildings that suffered some structural damage. Looming before us was the Golden Gate Bridge. What an awesome sight. Frank was looking forward to visiting Alcatraz, but it was temporarily closed. One of our excursions took us to wine country. Even though I do not enjoy the taste of wine, I did appreciate the beauty of the vineyards. After leaving San Francisco, we headed down to Los Angeles. As we drove, I was in awe at the view of the Pacific Coast. When we arrived in Los Angeles, Frank and his brother had to put in a couple of days work. This was also when Frank began his transformation. Suddenly his personality began to change, especially toward me. Looking back, I now wonder if I was a welcome addition on this trip or if I was becoming a thorn in Frank's side. He began acting very suspicious. What was he hiding? In an attempt to lessen the friction, I became even nicer to Frank. Ironically, the kinder I was, the meaner he became. Regardless of Frank's apparent contempt toward me, I still enjoyed many attractions. We were lucky to see Johnny Carson host *The Late Show*, which happened to be one of his anniversary performances. A huge fan of *Days of our Lives*, I was right next to their studio. San Diego was our next stop. I was thrilled that we would be going to the zoo. Being such an animal lover, I marveled at the variety of animals this zoo housed. During the last leg of the trip, we went to Mexico. I fell in love with the blankets that the people in this country handmade. Frank fell in love with the tequila. I was really beginning to notice the problem he had, even though he vehemently denied it. You see, I was a target for Frank when he drank. His friends saw him in a lighter note. To them, Frank was the life of the party.

After our trip, I discovered a noticeable change in Frank. Forever the optimist, I thought we could work it out. As the holidays approached, I looked forward to our traditional Christmas dinner over at my in-laws. Frank added a glitch to our plans. He wanted

35

to spend this year alone with only our family. It was almost like he wanted to cause me misery. He knew how much I enjoyed the holidays, and spending it with family was an important element. New Year's Eve was not any better. Frank and I decided to have a small gathering of friends at our house to ring in the New Year. However, there was one major dilemma. Right before midnight, Frank disappeared. Ignorant to his whereabouts, I tried to behave naturally and entertain my guests. When Frank finally returned, he lashed out at me. He blamed me for putting a damper on his evening. Perhaps my distaste for his alcohol abuse was becoming more evident, and Frank did not appreciate my accusing eyes. Our fighting led to his departure. He was becoming awfully good at this. It was almost like he was looking for an excuse to get away from me, and I did not believe he was thinking about reconciling and making up. Again, I was questioning his actions.

Perhaps Frank and I just needed a break. You know what they say, "Absence makes the heart grow fonder." We decided that Maryanne and I would fly north to Rhode Island to visit family for a week. Hopefully, our time apart would reaffirm Frank's love for me and heighten our need to be together. Calling him every evening, I began to doubt that Frank even missed us. He seemed so cold and distant. It was a struggle to enjoy my family because my thoughts were on my marriage. Even eating was becoming a battle. Swallowing food becomes impossible when there is a huge knot in your stomach. Eager to get home, I wanted to run into my husband's loving arms at the airport. Certainly, he would welcome Maryanne and me with open arms. Surprisingly, we were greeted by an imposter. Frank strolled into the airport donning a pair of sunglasses. How strange to be wearing glasses indoors. He was so aloof toward us. This was a far cry from what I expected. I began to wonder if he wished we had stayed up north. Hiding behind darkened lenses, Frank would not look me in the eye. At this moment, I felt my world was beginning to fall apart.

4

Pulling into the driveway, I sensed that something was not quite right. I could not shake off this uneasy premonition. Upon entering the garage, I immediately noticed that the room in the basement which once housed furniture was now empty. I felt like I had been kicked in the gut. The pool table and furnishings were gone. Either we had been robbed, or my husband owed me an explanation. I think I would have preferred the first scenario. However, my husband decided to come clean. While I was away, he had found an apartment to live in. He thought he needed space to think, time alone. He was confused about his future. My body was in shock. Sadly, he was doing this to Maryanne and me. I was so sure of my love for him and thought he felt the same.

Still in disbelieve, I followed him upstairs. I cried as he packed his clothing. Begging him to stay, my pleas were ignored. Obviously, Frank had already made up his mind. To make matters worse, he would not even tell me where he was living. Upset and alone, I called my parents when he left. They advised me to call a lawyer as soon as possible. Knowing I had to confide in my in-laws, I dialed their number next. In the past, Frank has tried to sicken their perception of me. Frank tried to convince them that I was the guilty one, always putting him down. Thankfully, they were wise enough to realize that their son had a serious issue and it was not his wife. The demon that Frank was dealing with was the bottle. It was comforting to know that they saw through his lies and supported me.

On Monday morning, I followed my families' advice and contacted a divorce lawyer. I was told that he would require a retainer fee of $4,000. Since my husband controlled the finances, I did not have access to this sum of money. Remarkably, my in-laws came to my rescue. They gave me the money, and I continued to seek legal counsel. I was informed of my spousal rights. Frank would be responsible for child support as well as alimony. I'm sure he would regret wanting me to stay home for the last five years. His desire to control me and my life was now coming back to haunt him. Scared, I knew that I would have to go back to school if I intended on supporting Maryanne and myself in the future. I had so many plans to make but lacked the confidence to do it alone. I just assumed that Frank would always be in our lives, supporting us and keeping a roof over our heads. The lawyer advised me to stay away from my husband. I knew that Frank's controlling personality would make his wishes impossible. The locks of the doors were changed, but I still let him in. He was trying to reassure me that he was not involved with anyone else, and I desperately wanted to believe him. As hard as it was for even me to swallow, I still wanted my spouse home. I set out intending to win back his love.

Occasionally, Frank would stop by to visit. This was my chance to woo him back with romantic subtleties. I would create an aura of tranquility with candles and set the table with wine and cheese. Frank was a willing participant but would leave each evening to return to his apartment. Desperate to have my old life back, I was willing to enable and support my husband's habits. In essence, my behavior was justifying his actions and falsely made me the guilty party. Here I was suffering, unable to eat or sleep and Frank was as happy as a clam.

My confusion led me to seek support from my priest. Unfortunately, he did not provide much comfort. Frank had made the decision to leave, and the church could not force him to return. Marriage needed a commitment by both partners and right now, one of the players was not cooperating. Morally, the church does not condone Frank's decision but legally, there was nothing I could do.

Frank agreed to go to counseling, but I quickly realized that it was a waste of time. He went through the motions, but his heart was not in it. In order for this to work, Frank needed to admit that he had a problem and issues that he needed to deal with. He convinced himself and everyone else that I was the one who needed to change. He just needed time to work out his feelings. Internally I shouted, *What about mine?* To mask my emotional torment, I physically decided to change. After losing twenty pounds, I began to feel better about myself. If I looked good on the outside, I would begin to feel better inside. Certainly, Frank would find me irresistible and come crawling back. I foolishly planned our date nights, reaffirming Frank's notions that he was special and I could not live without him. Even my neighbors knew about our marital woes. It was no longer a secret. Unashamed, I was hell-bent on winning back my husband, even if some thought I was ridiculous.

Frank continued to insist that he was not involved with another woman. Like most women, I wanted to believe this or, should I say, needed to believe this. My self-esteem, the little I had, would be crushed if I found out otherwise. My lawyer recommended that I hire a private investigator to follow Frank. My father generously sent me a thousand dollars to pay for this service. I was hoping that it would be money wasted and my husband was forthright. One evening went by with Frank being tailed, and the investigator had nothing to report. No news was good news. However, my lawyer called me the following evening to report different findings. Apparently, Frank was seen leaving his apartment, and he was not alone. He was with another woman. A wave of relief washed over me. I actually felt better knowing the truth. Now I knew what I was dealing with. Knowing Frank was with another woman, I intended to get even. I called his answering machine and left a recording that I hoped both would hear, "Hi Frank, I just wanted to call and thank you for such a romantic evening the other night!" I wanted this other woman to feel what I was experiencing. She would also know that Frank was two-timing her. How crazy. Even though she and I were the victims, I was lashing out at the wrong person. Frank should have been targeted. Calling my lawyer the next day, I decided that I had enough. Frank was served divorce papers, and we would go our separate ways. This sounded simple enough, but Frank had other intentions.

I didn't tell Frank that I had him followed. I just told him that a divorce was a reasonable alternative to our rocky marriage. Obviously, he wasn't happy, and neither was I. Frank was upset when he was served the papers. I do not believe he thought I would ever go through with it. This realization made him change his attitude, and he begged me to take him back. He admitted that there was someone else, but he did not love her. He had even foolishly bought her a ring. Apparently, his drinking and partying led to this not his true feelings. He wanted to break off this relationship and come back to me. Three months had passed since Frank left, but it felt like an eternity. I had been living in limbo and was ready to put my life back in order. I wasn't ready to throw in the towel. I forgave him even though he was still partying. It was silly for me to think that circumstances would improve without Frank's complete submission. He was only putting a Band-Aid on his problem. He wasn't being honest with himself. Infidelity was not the issue. Frank's messed up head was the real problem. Booze was the culprit which caused his mind to be poisoned, which led to his actions.

Still living in the apartment, Frank and I decided to work on our marriage. He had signed a six month lease and thought it would be best to move slowly. I agreed. I would need time to heal from this devastation. My body was still numb.

Throughout this entire ordeal, I never engaged in a relationship with someone of the opposite sex, nor did I go out with any friends. My focus was strictly on rekindling my marriage and bringing Frank home. Attending church regularly, I was reminded that infidelity was a sin, and I would not be able to justify such actions in God's eyes. Regardless of Frank's moral decision, I was taught to forgive, but unfortunately, I could not forget what had been done to me. There were so many questions left unanswered, and only Frank had the key to unlock the uncertainties. In a sense, he chose to bury the past, showing only a glimmer of remorse. I expected so much more. For me, my marriage vows were sacred. On the other hand, Frank seemed to take them less seriously. Even though we were married so young, I found it hard to excuse his behavior based on maturity. My husband needed to grow up and accept responsibility for his actions or else he would continue to self-destruct. I would be left to pick up the pieces.

Life began to renew once Frank returned. The summer months were upon us, and friends began coming over to enjoy our pool and hospitality. Considerate of our privacy, guests did not speak of our problems, nor offer any opinions. Perhaps they did not know what to say or simply did not want to get involved. Either way, I was happy to move on. Surprisingly, my life took on another twist. I was late for my period, and I immediately took a pregnancy test. As fate would have it, we were having another baby. Of course, there were some who thought I intentionally got pregnant to entrap Frank, and there were some who had the audacity to question the father. They even tried to fill Frank's head with these lies. However, I knew this was a farce. Sure, I wanted another baby, but I would have preferred if our lives were more stable. How dare they question my integrity.

They were blaming me and not Frank, and he did not even have the decency to support me from these accusations. Finding it difficult to get excited with all these questions swarming in my head, I knew this baby deserved a happy mom. Like any birth, this was a gift from God, and it was time to change my attitude. My new focus was geared toward my health, and I began to concentrate on the miracle growing inside me. That was a much better alternative.

Frank continued to work, which involved a lot of traveling and time away from home. My body continued to grow with pregnancy and a lot of food. Perhaps I was eating for comfort rather than nourishment. Knowing that Frank's issues were not resolved, I found it difficult to be at peace, and food became a crutch. I couldn't smoke or drink, but I certainly could eat without harming the fetus. So that is exactly what I did! I was looking forward to an upcoming trip to Myrtle Beach. This year, we were spending Thanksgiving there along with my in-laws. By this time, they had purchased a three-bedroom home located near the ocean. My parents had also purchased a home in the same development. Myrtle Beach had grown into a vacation spot for both families, and for this, I am very thankful.

Ordinarily I would not have been upset that Frank decided to go to a football game at UGA with a friend. I would expect that he would go to the game and come directly home afterwards. After all I had been through, this wasn't asking too much. Apparently Frank wanted to exert his masculinity and called at 11:00 p.m. . Trying to be civil, I asked him when he would be home. His reply, "I'll get there when I get there." I guess Frank needed to remind me that he was the boss. He had nothing to be sorry about, and he did not intend to butter me up.

When Christmas rolled around, the aura was much different this year. Bill was now single and alone, and Steve, Frank's youngest brother, now had a daughter and son. I can remember looking at envy at Steve and his loved ones. To me, they represented the perfect family. I admired the adoration and attention Steve bestowed upon his wife and children. There was no denying that they came first. As my children grew, I would often share motherly advice. Marrying a husband like Uncle Steve, I thought, was wise and would often suggest this to my daughters. He didn't have any skeletons hiding in the closet, or so I thought.

My due date was right around the corner. Soon February came, and we began anticipating our new arrival. I was rightfully convinced that Maryanne, now four and a half years old, would be a marvelous big sister. Forgoing the natural method, I decided that this birth would be tolerated with some pain medication. Therefore, the doctors administered an epidermal when I was four centimeters dilated. Not needing to be a hero, I was pleased that I did not experience much pain this time. Mindy entered the world as perfect as any baby could be. With a head full of curly black hair, she was the cutest infant. What I noticed immediately were the dimples on her cheeks. Knowing that they came from Frank, I smiled. My beautiful daughter would not be here if I had not taken her father back. By giving him a second chance, I was blessed with another miracle. Seeing the love in Maryanne's eyes, I knew that things would be better for her. She now had a sister to love and play with. For this, I have no regrets.

5

While bathing my baby on Easter morning, I remember thinking how lucky I was and how grateful I was for all the blessings God had given me. Even though my life had its share of hardships, I was also granted many privileges. That day, I would celebrate the holy day with family enjoying a wonderful meal prepared at a fancy hotel. I was not alone, and I would not go hungry like so many. I must never forget my share of happy memories, for they would give me the strength to overcome the difficult times. You know what they say, "You must accept the good along with the bad." My life has been a testament to this cliché.

Frank had booked a cruise for him and me to Nassau in the Bahamas. Realizing that we needed some time alone, I agreed to this trip. Even though Mindy was only three months old, she was in good hands. I knew my in-laws would take excellent care of our children. On our first evening, Frank and I met another couple, and we spent most of our time together. This was not my idea of a romantic getaway. A beer-drinking contest was not part of my itinerary. Not surprisingly, Frank won the award. Beaming with pride, my husband acted like he was presented with the Nobel Peace

Prize. To be honest, I was more disgusted than proud. After four days, I was more than ready to go home. I was eager to see my new baby. Perhaps Frank had planned this trip a little too soon after her birth. Finally I might be able to relax and let my hair down without feeling edgy.

Summer came, and I was thrilled to be going to Myrtle Beach to spend time with my sisters and family. I had rejoined the gym to shed a few pounds. Sisters can be so critical. I had also managed to make a few friends. My life basically revolved around Frank. I found some solace being at the gym and at church. This was my opportunity to form my own identity and forge relationships with people that I had something in common with. Most of Frank's friends liked to drink, and all of our activities included alcohol. Unfortunately, I anticipated that our trip to Myrtle Beach would mimic the same behavior. Frank would spend most of the week drinking, oblivious that this was a family trip. The center of Frank's attention was an alluring bottle, not his family. I still managed to have a good time, regardless of him. I would not let him effect the little time I had with my family, even if it took every ounce of energy I had to remain positive.

Frank would be turning thirty in July, and my friends and I were planning a big party. The theme of it was a Hawaiian Luau. A pig was roasted in a pit overnight while Frank and his friends sat around watching it cook. Of course this required some beverages. Frank always found an excuse to drink. Porta-Johns were in place, and the band was rocking on our deck. For a laugh, I hired a motorcycle mama to perform for Frank. I videotaped much of the party so that we could reminisce in the future. Frank's family was able to come and enjoy. Disappointed, I knew my family could not attend. Our visits had to be planned, not spontaneous. This was a major drawback in my decision to move one thousand miles away, one I had not considered.

Frank continued to make plans with his friends. Together, we hosted several NASCAR parties. Generous with food and drinks, our parties were always a great success. My husband was quick to make jokes and always the life of the party. Full of energy during the festivities, Frank didn't run out of steam until the last guest left. To my displeasure, he turned the other cheek when it came to assisting me in cleaning up. Sitting leisurely in *his* recliner, Frank slept while I worked. At times, I felt like hired help or, should I say, the dutiful wife. Carrying the recycling bin to the end of the driveway for garbage pickup required a lot of agility. The overflowing bin could easily topple over and beer cans would spew over if I was not careful. Sarcasm was not usually a trait I liked to portray. However, frustration can lead to undesirable characteristics when you feel like your being taken advantage of.

For Frank and me, our life became a vicious circle. We would begin drinking and partying. Soon after, fights between us would break out and eventually this would lead to reconciliation. While we did not physically abuse each other, the verbal abuse was horrific. Putting each other down became second nature and acceptable. We both failed to see the irreparable damage our words could have for ourselves and children. It is not fun living in a hostile environment. I did not enjoy the shouting matches I heard as a child growing up in my home. Why did I think my children would feel any differently?

Living with stress became part of my daily routine. I sought ways to relieve the tension by working out at the gym and venting. I quickly discovered that I was not the only one facing turmoil in a marriage. This knowledge somewhat lessened the aguish I was feeling. Realizing I was not alone gave me a source of strength, but honesty also caused some conflict. There were some that were perplexed by my so-called stupidity. My sister would also be there to listen to my woes, but she also felt it was necessary to voice her opinion about her apparent dislike of my lifestyle. Frank thought that she was attempting to manipulate my thoughts. This caused friction between my sister and husband and at times, their resentment toward each other played out. I felt I had to choose between two people that I loved, and this was sad. Nobody should have to make this choice. Perhaps if I lived in Rhode Island with my entire family's support, things may have been different. I wasn't secure enough in myself to do it alone, recognizing that financially and emotionally I still needed Frank.

Rhode Island still held some very fond memories and thankfully was still a part of my life. I still cherish the times we traveled there for Christmas when the children were young. Nothing can compare to a traditional Italian Christmas. Nobody left the table hungry. I smile when I watch the videotapes of my children and their cousins opening their presents and melt when I see their excitement. As Visa would say, "These times are priceless." Looking back, I regret the fact that I took this for granted when I was younger. I never thought I would miss these times in the future, for I only wanted to grow up and be independent. If I could turn back time, I would have truly cherished my childhood. I have learned to live in the moment because each second is precious, and the time you have with loved ones will not last forever.

Mindy's second birthday rolled around, and the party was planned. However, I had more on my mind that day than simply being the perfect hostess. I mentioned to my sister that I was two days late for my period. She volunteered to come by in the morning to collect a urine sample from me. She would have it tested that day. When the phone rang that morning, I anxiously answered. My sister began singing "Rock-a-bye Baby." I knew what she was inferring but didn't know whether I should laugh or cry. I was happy to have a life growing inside of me, but at the same time, I was in shock. I never expected to conceive so easily without even trying. Financially, Frank's company was doing well. However, I knew raising three children would put a strain on our finances. Also, I did not anticipate any help around the house from Frank. I had grown accustomed to completing all the household duties. Deciding to remain positive, I was resolved to enjoy this last pregnancy to the fullest. I did not have to put my children in daycare, I was able to exercise and take care of myself, and I wasn't worried about paying bills. How dare I complain when life could be so much worse.

I switched my gynecologist so that I could have my sister as a nurse. I was fortunate to have so many ultrasounds, yet we were unable to determine this baby's gender. Deep down, I was not disappointed. I still looked forward to being surprised until the baby came. Marissa arrived early on October 11. This delivery was so quick that I almost did not make it to the hospital. I was ten centimeters dilated when I arrived. My doctor was across the street shopping at the Home Depot. Thankfully, he was able to rush right over. This baby had no intention of waiting. Painful yet worth it, I had another healthy baby girl to cherish. Despite my religious upbringing, I had my tubes tied immediately after this baby. In this decision, my head won out over my heart. Unfortunately, Frank's partying had not slowed down. Raising three children can be burdensome for any family. In my family, I was basically doing it alone. Most of the time, Frank was not in any condition to help out.

It was becoming more and more obvious that Frank was the king of the castle. He demanded control and called all the shots. I needed his approval for most of the purchasing and recreational decisions. Frank was notorious for putting himself first. I, on the other hand, found pleasure in making others happy. It seems kind of crazy that two people can be so different yet married. I guess opposites really do attract, but would they eventually repel?

Frank's family was so quiet and private. I was not used to this because my own family made their issues quite public. I chose to keep friends at bay when I was growing up. I had my share of socializing but rarely at my home. My parents' constant yelling and a house with three other sisters was too much volume and caused much embarrassment. Now here I was, reliving the same atmosphere and causing my children the same stress. Frank and I would scream at each other. Name calling was common between us, and the vocabulary we chose was not appropriate. I tried to talk to the kids about this and would tell them how wrong this was, but yet I continued to let it happen. What a hypocrite I was becoming. Poor Maryanne was a witness to this at the age of ten. She was old enough to know what was going on, and I'm sure she was affected by it. I did my best to create alternative happy memories for her. I made my children my life, and we were always together. Busy with CCD classes, church, and softball, my children and I were living day by day the best that we could with or without their father.

One evening, Frank and I were invited to a Halloween party. An old friend who was once our neighbor was throwing a party. The neighborhood was approximately forty-five minutes away. Looking forward to seeing old friends, Frank and I decided to go. The drive home was a fiasco. I knew that Frank and I were both guilty of consuming some alcohol. However, I did not realize the severity of this, nor did I question his ability to drive. Evidently I was wrong. Stunned, I saw flashing lights behind our vehicle, and they were intended for us. The cop was privy to something, and made Frank submit to a breathalyzer test. He was way over the legal limit. He was arrested, and he would not be able to drive home. The cop then asked me to also take a test. Thankfully, I only registered 0.6— not legally drunk. The cop insisted that I take the wheel and drive myself home. In complete denial, we still had a NASCAR party the following day. Obviously, we had not learned a lesson and continued to think we were invincible. We had gotten away with it this time. Frank would not take blame and instead tried to convince me that I was at fault. I should have known better and driven. If we could turn back the clock, perhaps I would have.

6

In 1995 Maryanne and I were taking a trip to Savannah with her
Girl Scout troop. I had to leave Mindy, who was five, and Marissa,
who was two, at home with their father. This wouldn't worry most
mothers, but I felt uneasy. I was hoping that Frank would take the
reins and be Mr. Mom. When we arrived home, I did not witness
anything earth shattering. Basically, Frank had done a fair job. I
cannot say I was pleased to find Frank's drinking buddy there when
we came home, but the children were fine and that was really all
that mattered. Yes, I wished things were different, but I didn't know
how to change them. Frank continued to drink; he associated with
friends who also drank, and I tried to hold it all together by being a
good mother and trying to be civil. I believed that it was best for my
family to stay united and hoped my mothering was enough to get us
by. My only alternative was to leave my husband, take the girls, and
try to raise them as a single mom. I was not confident that I could
do so successfully.

There I was contemplating the future of my marriage, and Frank
asked me to renew our marriage vows. After some thought and soul
searching, I too was looking forward to a new beginning. Perhaps

this would be a good idea and a chance to rekindle some feelings of commitment that had been lost over the tumultuous years. After all, Frank had broken our wedding vows, and I believed this time our ceremony would be more special. Three beautiful girls, a tribute to our success, were there to help us celebrate. My family couldn't come because of the short notice, but Frank's family was able to attend. I asked my priest to conduct the ceremony, and I was thankful he agreed. The hours before leaving for church were quite disheartening. True to form, Frank decided to treat himself to a couple of cocktails, an idea I never considered. I began to question my decision. *Perhaps I should not bother going through with this.* Thinking about my family and their disappointment, I decided to let things slide. After our vows were exchanged, we treated our guests to dinner. I wish I had warm memories of this sacred ceremony, but sadly I don't. I knew this was something we needed to do, a step in the right direction, yet I was hoping that this day would have been different and Frank could have been sober.

I began to notice that my oldest dog seemed ill. Because she had been on steroids for most of her life for skin allergies, the doctor thought her liver was failing. This was devastating. I knew that we would inevitably have to put her down. Bringing her to the vet for the last time was heart wrenching. Not only would we miss her, but her daughter would be alone. I hated the fact that she lived such a short life. I never truly got over the loss of any of my pets. This was something I just learned to live with.

Around this time, my best friend and I were planning a pocketbook party. Designer purses were a hot commodity, and women were eager to have them. Imitation or fake purses were being sold at a more reasonable cost. Unaware of Gucci, Coach, and other designer labels, I thought this sounded like fun. It was also my chance to get together with some girls—friends of mine, not Frank's. Unfortunately, he was not so excited. A ruckus broke out in my backyard while I was setting up for the party. Frank became

A DANGEROUS COMBINATION

extremely belligerent toward me. Perhaps he did not like the idea that I had some control. He wasn't calling the shots for this party, and he did not like it. This time, I refused to back down. I was having my party with or without his approval.

Frank had decided to take the girls to a pet store to look for a new dog. Without my knowledge or consent, they chose a Black Lab. My love for dogs is unwavering, but Frank was very selfish not to include me in this decision. This large breed would require a lot of space and care. Being that I was the sole caretaker, I didn't really appreciate this burden. Instead of welcoming this new puppy into my home, I greeted him and my family with anger. How dare he do this to me! Cursing and yelling in front of the children, this was far from a Kodak moment. Quickly, this puppy found his way into my heart. While I was cooking dinner that evening, he laid his head upon my feet. My anger soon turned to love. Sure, I was still disappointed in Frank's lack of concern for my feelings, but it wasn't the dog's fault. However, I can tell you that he was to blame for other actions. To name a few: chewing the lights around the pool, gnawing on speaker wires, and changing the look of our fence. Unfortunately he didn't improve the value of these items. I could have said, "I told you so," but I didn't. Instead, I grew to love my dog and appreciated his loyalty, obedience, and companionship. As a matter of fact, he became my new walking buddy.

Every Sunday the girls and I would attend Mass. On one particular Sunday, the priest mentioned during the sermon that help was needed to deliver meals to those needing assistance. With Marissa beginning preschool, I knew I would have some time available. I offered to volunteer the first Thursday of every month. At this point in my life, I truly began to realize how fortunate I was and felt I needed to give back. There were so many people in this world that had less than me. I had a roof over my head, food on my table, and three healthy children. I always tried to see the glass as being half full. Instead of focusing on the negative aspects of my life, I chose

DEROUIN & DIROCCO

52

to relish in the positive. Delivering meals to people so that they would not go hungry made me feel good about myself. In all my years on this earth, I have never gone hungry. For this I am blessed.

Friends and family were now recognizing that Frank had a drinking problem. On one of my parents' visits to Georgia, my father confronted me about this issue. I didn't deny the truth, but I failed to admit the severity. Unfortunately my parents did not hold the magic wand to make the problem disappear. I do not believe they really understood what alcoholism was; therefore, they could not suggest any solutions.

On occasion Frank would go golfing with some of his buddies. After a round of golf one day, Frank was entering our cul-de-sac in his car. Evidently alcohol had skewed his driving abilities, and he took down my neighbor's mailbox. The issue was easily solved. He was asked to simply replace the mailbox. This neighbor was also a big drinker. I'm sure he thought the situation was no big deal. Thankfully, nobody had gotten hurt. Frank also spent a lot of time golfing with his dad. It did not matter where or with whom he was playing; Frank always included alcohol with his game. His dad would not admit that Frank's drinking was serious. Instead, he chose to brush it under the rug. He was still doing well on the job, and together, he and his dad had grown a successful company. My husband had become a working alcoholic; therefore he was not perceived as bad. However, my perception was quite different.

I started to confront Frank about his excessive drinking. I attempted to scare him by threatening to leave him if he refused to stop. Unfortunately, Frank did not show any concern. He knew I had no place to go. Seeing I had been out of the workforce for ten years, I did not feel I had any credentials to offer prospective employers. I didn't have a college degree or any expertise to support me. In addition, he realized I lacked the support of my family. Basically, I was stuck. The idea of not being able to provide for my children frightened me, and Frank took advantage of my insecurities. Realizing now the importance of independence, I try to relay this to my girls now. Becoming self-sufficient was not in my future because my financial needs were so tied to Frank. He was not the type to pay alimony and child support willingly, and I knew this. Trapped, I chose to focus on the love I had for my husband rather than the reasons I could not live with him. I was unable to shelter the girls from the verbal abuse I suffered, but I hope they are never targeted with such words. It was my goal to provide my children with the ammunition they would need for adulthood. I strove to give them a college education, and if this meant I needed to suffer, then I was willing to do so. If I left Frank, I knew my family would struggle and college would be a remote possibility. I wanted them to have all that I had done without. Some may think I was being selfish; I try to think that I was being selfless.

Many viewed my family with envy. To the outside world, we looked like the picture of happiness. Our snapshot was a hard-working, successful husband, dutiful wife, and three beautiful girls. Nobody would expect that a family trip to the Tennessee Mountains would hold sorrowful memories. I have those wonderful pictures to share of our family enjoying the breathtaking scenery. We had an adorable photograph taken of the entire family decked out in Western attire. Looking at this picture today, I cherish the good times we had. Thus far, Frank had stuck to his promise and remained sober. On the last night of our vacation the pressure, or perhaps withdrawal, became too much for him to handle. After purchasing a twelve pack of beer, Frank managed to drink every one. Thankfully, my children did not remember this part of the trip. I'm glad the memories are only in my head, because a drunken father is not a pretty sight and a photograph they could do without.

When we returned home, my younger sister and her two children came to Georgia for a visit. She too was having marital problems. Totally understanding and relating to her woes, I wasn't going to allow this to get in the way of our time together. I was determined to show her a good time. Heck, I was a veteran. My oldest sister was throwing a fortieth birthday party for her husband. A couple of other men were also celebrating their birthdays. She and her friends decided to throw one big party together. The neighborhood pool was the perfect setting to gather. They also had access to grills and a clubhouse. I looked forward to an evening of entertainment and fun. I wasn't prepared for what occurred. This was definitely an adult party. The alcohol was plentiful, and the entertainment was risqué. Two female strippers were hired to perform for the birthday boys. I imagined that they would strip and leave. Boy, was I naïve. They began to perform lap dances. Shocked and embarrassed, I thought this was disgusting. Obviously, my younger sister and I were the only ones disappointed. Everyone else, including Frank, seemed to enjoy their performance. Call me a moral prude, but I could not condone this behavior. Between Frank's apparent pleasure in viewing this and the fact that he was sneaking drinks, I was completely pissed off. Once again, I attempted to hide my displeasure for my sister's benefit. Our time together was limited, and I wanted to enjoy every moment. It wasn't my party to plan. I was only a guest and could leave if I wanted to. The problem was I would be leaving alone because it was evident that Frank was not ready to go. Perhaps if I closed my eyes, the atmosphere would disappear, and I could pretend to have a good time. Thankfully, it was dark out, and my facial expressions would not give away my true feelings. What I did notice was the look on my oldest sister's face. Apparently, she was happy and really, that was what mattered most. I swallowed my pride and made it through the evening. I learned that I could still have my opinions and follow my own moral guidelines without being influenced. I stayed but did not partake in the festivities. Some may have thought that I was a party pooper, but I did not care. They too needed to respect my opinion; now if only I could get Frank to.

Soon after my sister left, Frank and I got into a heated argument. Knowing that it was best to separate before matters got any worse, I locked myself in my bedroom. We both needed to cool off. Frank did not appreciate my aloofness and began to bang on the bedroom door. Punching so hard, he put a hole through the wood. This was the first time Frank had damaged something out of anger, and I was scared. I grabbed the girls and took them to Chick-fil-A to gather my thoughts. Adding to my discomfort, my daughter Mindy had a friend over. Poor Mindy, she must have been so uncomfortable. However, she acted like a trooper and never complained. They seemed to be adjusting to their father's outbursts. Like me, they figured that this was somewhat normal. Returning home, I gathered some belongings for the girls and me and went to spend the night with my in-laws. Calling the next morning, Frank was apologetic. He promised to make things better. He told me he would rush off to Home Depot to buy a new door. The broken door was not the cause of my departure. The reason for my leaving was his behavior, and the cause was his drinking. The effect of this was now tangible. Frank could witness the damage right before his eyes. My broken spirit was truly evident.

Time passed, and my life continued on the same path. Maryanne had been playing softball, and I was able to enjoy the games. I loved sitting on the bleachers and cheering her team on. I wished I could say the same for Frank. When he did come, which was not very often, the smell of booze escaped his mouth. He did not even have the decency to frequent his daughter's game sober. Approaching forty, Frank would surely outgrow this behavior. Unfortunately, I failed to realize that this addiction was controlling him. Like I had mentioned previously, I was unfamiliar about alcoholism and believed that he could stop if he wanted to. In addition, his brother Bill was reconciling with his wife and was getting remarried in Hawaii. Happy for them, I thought that Frank would wake up too and want to rekindle our marriage. He needed to count his blessings and quickly divert from this path of self-destruction. Surely this successful businessman could control his destiny. He was allowing a substance to dictate his fate.

In an effort to save money and feel a sense of accomplishment, I would often take charge of projects in our home. I enjoyed wallpapering and painting the walls in the house. Focusing on Mindy's bedroom, I had begun painting her room. Taking a break, I hid out in the backyard to smoke a cigarette. Smoking was a habit that I did not want my children to observe. Finishing, I extinguished the butt and returned inside to continue working. My youngest daughter came running into the bedroom yelling, "Mommy, the backyard is on fire!" Dropping the paintbrush, I dashed downstairs and looked out the bay window in my kitchen. Smoke was billowing from the pine straw. I grabbed the hose from my backyard and luckily was able to put the flames out. The fire had damaged some pine straw and blackened a portion of the fence. Quickly, I fixed the pine straw and painted the fence before Frank returned home. I was frightened that if he found out, he would scream. It did not take much to trigger Frank's anger. I had to convince Marissa that this was our secret. To this day, I have never shared this story with Frank. I am just thankful that on that day Marissa was my guardian angel. I have my children's trust and devotion, and they have mine. During all our misery, we always had each other.

Realizing I also needed the strength of God, I would listen to the whispers ringing in my ears when I was in church or when I felt weak. On one particular Sunday, his voice became loud, and my faith was being tested. I was asked if I was interested in teaching CCD. I was reassured that this would be an opportunity learn about my faith and pass this knowledge onto little ones. To seal the deal, I would be able to teach Mindy, who was also in the first grade. I now had a second chance to learn about my faith since I had chosen to disregard this opportunity as a youngster. I owed this to my children and myself. Two wonderful and caring women were generous enough to help me along. One woman had a deep faith that I greatly admired. I prayed to God that one day I could model myself after her. Because of my decision, I grew in my religion and became a better worshipper. I continued my journey teaching CCD for many, many years.

I have always considered myself a giving person. Frank too was very generous with himself and others. He was always reaching into his pocket to show others a good time. His youngest brother had fallen upon hard times and needed to borrow ten thousand dollars. Frank felt he needed to share this with me in case something happened to him. He had worked out a monthly payment plan with his brother and reassured me that he would not renege on his promise. My perfect brother-in-law was showing signs that he was not invincible as I had once thought. Hopefully this was not a sign of things to come.

The millennium was upon us, and Frank was planning a New Year's party. The kids and I were looking forward to ringing in the New Year with friends. A few guests were invited including my husband's friend, our old neighbor. I had to put aside my feelings for him to make Frank happy. I knew that together they drank too much, but Frank promised that this time it would be different. When he returned from the liquor store with four gallons of alcohol, I questioned him. Did we really need all this booze for a few friends? He attempted to reassure me that this was also for the future. He just decided to stock up. Like usual, I believed him. Denial was so much easier then acceptance. The party turned out to be a success.

7

Hopeful, I looked forward to the new millennium. The world was excited, and I desperately wanted to share in the enthusiasm. In an attempt to stay positive, I did not dwell on the past and focused on the future. Currently, I was dealing with my husband's abuse of alcohol, but I was thankful that I had the love and support of his family. A source of comfort, his family was always there when I needed them. I never expected that a member of Frank's family would lead to his further demise. As I had mentioned earlier, I adored and admired Frank's youngest brother. Steve was the epitome of goodness, reliance, and a role model partner. I envied his wife and admired their relationship. Often, I questioned Frank's self-righteousness because of his decision to drink. Placing Steve on a pedestal, I never expected him to sway or display any immoral or questionable behavior. Boy, I was in for a surprise. Evidently Steve had been stealing money from my family. Frank had lent him ten thousand dollars before. Now, he had unknowingly swindled him. He devised a plan to retrieve blank checks that credit cards were sending to Frank. He would forge Frank's name on these checks and cash them for his own personal use. Every month, Steve would pay the minimum payment due on the cash advances. His plan backfired when Frank discovered his indiscretion. Altogether Steve successfully put us thousands of dollars in debt. Angry and in disbelief, Frank confronted his brother demanding an explanation. Steve simply stated that he was short on making his bills each month and needed the extra money. Frank's dad accepted his explanation and wrote us a check to cover Steve's expenses. Steve promised to pay him back and the issue was brushed under the rug. My instincts told me that there was more to this story but for now, I had to be satisfied with Steve's rendition.

Searching for the leftover alcohol from New Year's Eve, I discovered that there wasn't anything left but empty bottles. Unfortunately I knew who the culprit was and confronted him when he returned home from work. As usual, Frank was ready with excuses. Apparently, he was so distraught over his brother's antics that he found solace in drinking. He promised to stop immediately. I figured that this was a normal reaction and that, indeed, Frank was entitled to some relief. I was happy that he was forging ahead and that the shock was over. To ensure that Frank was unable to consume so much alcohol, I suggested that gallons of alcohol were not wise, nor should they be available in our home. Frank readily agreed and offered his own advice. He thought that a few glasses of wine at dinner were appropriate, and unconvinced, I agreed. Truthfully, I would have been happier if he had said no alcohol, but I was willing to give it a try. Surely, many couples shared wine with their dinner. However, Frank's idea of a few glasses turned into an entire bottle. So much for a compromise, I thought. Once again, Frank was calling the shots, and I enabled him to do so.

Frank's parents were ignorant to the fact that their son had a serious issue. During one of our visits to Myrtle Beach, their eyes were opened, and they too were concerned that Frank's drinking had progressed beyond social. After a day and night of partying, Frank became quite belligerent and a fight ensued. On this particular occasion, a loud battle broke out between us. Frank began screaming and ranting that we were leaving now! Waking up, his parents were confronted with a very drunk son and a daughter-in-law who was being victimized. Immediately, they spoke up in my defense. They told Frank that he was able to leave. However, the kids and I would be staying behind. This was the pinnacle that changed everything for his parents and me. From this point forward, I thought of them as my best friends and confidantes. I could rely on them to support me even if it meant turning on their son. I had them in my corner. They say that blood is thicker than water. In my case, I am happy that my in-laws rejected this notion. They were able to decipher right from wrong and were not ashamed to admit that their son was the latter. Hopefully, they could make him come to his senses. If only things could be that simplistic.

Arriving home from the beach, I decided to do a little investigation. Frank had the uncanny habit of visiting the basement. I knew that something had to be there that triggered these visits and was determined to discover what it was. My intuition brought me over to the bar. Removing the ceiling tiles, I uncovered several pint-size bottles of vodka. Frank had amassed quite a collection. Privy to his hiding place, I shared my discovery with Frank when he arrived home. He tried to lessen the severity of my accusations and told me that it was not a big deal. He wasn't hiding anything. These bottles had accumulated over a long period of time. Too bad I didn't believe him. Frank needed help, and I told him that if he wanted to stay with the kids and me, then he must seek counseling. I called my parents for support. Forcing Frank to speak with them, he promised both them and me that he would get help. Apparently, my threat was convincing enough to make Frank take action. Perhaps the kids and I were important and instrumental in his life. I was happy he chose to save our marriage.

Frank went outside to call a friend. I thought he was calling for advice and was okay with that. Sometimes we needed unbiased friends that we could lean on. However, my insecurities forced me to listen on the other side of the fence out of Frank's view. His conversation was ridiculing toward me, and he was completely unsympathetic to what had just transpired. Instead I heard Frank say, "What would Sandy think if she knew that my boss and I had just spent three hundred dollars at a strip joint while on a business trip in Texas?" My response was pure disgust and astonishment. Raging with contempt, I ran toward Frank and tried pushing him into the pool. I could tell by his voice that he was drinking and didn't want to confront him in a shouting match. Instead I sought revenge by ending his conversation with a splash. His friend would then know exactly what I thought of his escapades. At that moment, I wanted to ask Frank for a divorce, but I didn't. Instead, I asked myself if this was truly the solution I was seeking. Frank had made some terrible choices. These were his decisions, not mine. I needed to think about the consequence of divorce and what this would mean for my family and me. I always believed that two wrongs do not make something right, and I questioned the idea of uprooting my children without their consent. Left with too many questions, I was unable to pull the trigger.

Frank was resolved to give it a try and go to rehab. He began classes, which only lasted for a couple of weeks. Finally, my prayers were being answered. After completing the classes, Frank continued his recovery process by taking part in AA. While Frank was working toward healing, I knew that my suffering also needed attention. I joined Al-Anon for support. It was helpful to listen to others as they spoke about their experiences living with an alcoholic. I listened and learned a lot about what I needed to do to be successful and competent. They suggested that I separate my life from the alcohol by beginning a career outside my home. Thus far, my life had completely revolved around Frank and the children. This was a feeble attempt for independence. I began working for a pet sitting business. Frank was notorious for putting me down, and this was not an exception. However, I tried to ignore his ridicule and figured I could earn some money for the family. Subsequently, business was booming during Christmas. I had several jobs lined up while customers were traveling over the holiday. This did not sit well with Frank. He said that I was ruining our holiday and added that the income I earned was menial. We had horrendous fights throughout the holiday season. I came to the conclusion that it wasn't worth it. I was willing to forgo my job because I hated the atmosphere in my home, and I felt responsible. Once again Frank was in control, and I was forced to make changes and bend. I would have to seek advice from others at Al-Anon. Maybe there would be alternatives that would make me happy or, should I say, make Frank happy.

Things began looking up for my family while Frank abstained from drinking. Thankfully, he was a participant at AA almost daily. My sister-in-law Lynn had just given birth to her first baby. Unlike me, she was a working mother and asked if I was interested in babysitting for my nephew during the day while she worked. Sounding like a great idea, I quickly responded yes. I was looking forward to spending time with my new nephew and also earning some money. Frank and I had begun going out once a week on what we referred to as date nights. I was able to use my money for these evenings. It felt very rewarding contributing to the family finances. Even though it wasn't much, it was something.

While my life was beginning to calm, I was shaken by what was happening to our country. Watching *Good Morning America* on September 11, 2001, I was jolted when I witnessed an airplane crash into the Twin Towers. I had been on the phone with my best friend when this occurred. We questioned what was going on. Quickly we learned the facts, and sadly we responded. I knew then that my problems were trivial compared to the sorrow and helplessness felt by those affected. I still had my husband and family to love and cherish. More than ever, I was willing to fight for our happiness. I, unlike some, was given another chance. It would be selfish to waste this blessing.

It felt almost strange to plan a trip to Disney World while our country was suffering. However, the president begged the people to go on with their lives. If we didn't, the terrorists would win. Frank had a convention to attend in Florida, and we planned on making it a family trip. I was confident in the security of our country, and we went ahead with our plans. Besides, the kids were looking forward to this trip, and we didn't want to disappoint them. They had seen enough hardship over the past couple of years. My in-laws would also be attending the convention. It would be wonderful to share our time together, surrounded by joy and laughter. They too had suffered over the years as they watched their boys falter. I can only imagine their grief. You try so hard to raise your children the best you can. Sadly, they witnessed their sons make very grave mistakes and couldn't stop or protect them.

The memories of this trip were pleasant. Frank was not drinking, which only added to my delight. I also noticed that he was attempting to eat healthier. Perhaps he had hit rock bottom and was on an upward swing. I often heard people say that abusers must fall hard before they can begin recovery. I was hoping this was true for Frank. I was very thankful to share this experience with my family and in-laws. I noted that the lines were very short for most of the rides. I'm sure many families had cancelled their trip due to the events of September 11. I'm glad we threw caution to the wind and put our fears aside. I had such great faith in myself, my family, and my country. They say good will overcome evil. Thus far, it had.

Following our trip, I looked forward to Thanksgiving and Christmas. My sister, the realist, was quick to remind me that I must take one day at a time. I was hoping these days would never end. Frank continued his treatment by participating in AA; however, I had withdrawn from my Al-Anon classes. The classes for me were on Wednesday, and I was babysitting on that day. Justifying my absence, I felt Frank needed the help more than me. He was showing great progress and even began drawing. He was always artistic and used his gift to create pictures for our home. The holidays proved to be quite memorable. I firmly believed that everything was going to be all right. By eliminating alcohol from his life, Frank had given me renewed faith in our marriage and its duration.

I became interested in the prospect of substitute teaching because of my sister-in-law. She currently was a substitute teacher in the county we lived in. I realized that all I would need was to complete a two hour class and submit to a background check. Eventually, my sister-in-law would not need me to babysit. I figured this class would open the door to an alternative opportunity for me when the need arose. In the year 2002, I utilized the classes I had taken and became a substitute teacher in my school district. For many years to follow, I was called to fill in for absent teachers and found myself very comfortable and competent. A taste of independence was a great dose of medicine toward healing, and it felt nice knowing that people were requesting me and appreciated the work I performed.

The company Frank and his Dad started was dissolving. The company that they represented made them an offer. They wanted to buy out their company but still have Frank work directly for them. His father would be forced to retire, which was sad. I knew he wasn't really ready but financially, the offer was good and made economic sense. Bill was also asked to stay on and work for the reps. Frank would oversee sales in the Southeast, and Bill would be one of his salesmen. Unfortunately, Steve was not asked to stay on. He would have to find a job elsewhere. With the events that had transpired between him and Frank, perhaps it was best that they separated in business. I believe Frank was having a hard time placing his trust in Steve. It was time for a fresh start without the negative memories. The economy was fairly stable, and Steve would be able to find employment. Frank would not have to feel guilty about

Steve being without an income. Life was running smoothly for all of us, or so I thought.

Eager to see my family, I jumped at the opportunity to fly home during the Easter holiday. Frank had to travel on business to Massachusetts, so we turned it into a family trip. Using Frank's frequent fliers miles, the entire family was able to fly for free. Blessed, our family would be able to enjoy northern cuisine this Easter. I was looking forward to the endless courses and breaking bread with my relatives. They were pleased with Frank's appearance and demeanor since he had quit drinking. I was reassured that I had made the right decision by choosing to stand by him and move on with our lives as a family. For me, divorce was so final, whereas forgiveness could lead to a brighter future.

Steve's dishonesty was still plaguing our thoughts. Why would he need that amount of money? His lifestyle was not that lavish, and he made a fairly substantial salary. Frank and I discussed his love of the lottery but determined that the debt he would have incurred would not substantiate the amount he had stolen. The takeover with my husband's company had not yet occurred, and Frank was still able to see his brother daily. Somehow he was different. Remarkably, Steve had changed from the attentive husband toward his wife, Wendy, to an aloof stranger. Suspicious, Wendy was keenly aware that her husband was exhibiting strange behaviors. He would often talk on the phone for hours. He would not speak openly but would demand privacy. Evidently, he was hiding something. She had plans to scrutinize the phone bill when it arrived at the end of the month. She promised to call when she gathered the evidence. Bothered, we were all looking for answers.

A couple of days later, Wendy called over to my sister-in-law's house. I happened to be babysitting, while Lynn was working out of the house in her office downstairs. I kept the kids occupied while she worked. Apparently, a number appeared quite frequently on their phone bill that Wendy did not recognize. Given the number,

Lynn and I decided to call. Nervous, we didn't know what to expect. Fearful for her and the kids, I was worried for them. Lynn dialed the number, and I breathlessly listened on the other line. The voice on the other end left us both speechless. Expecting to hear a feminine, "Hello," we were surprised to be greeted by a male. His voice did have a feminine twang. Immediately, I pondered his masculinity. I was not ignorant to homosexuals and believed that the person at the other end of line was in fact gay. Confused, we called Wendy and shared our concerns. Curious, she also called the number and confirmed our findings. However, she chose to confront this stranger instead of hanging up. His response was nonchalant. He explained that he and Steve were merely friends. Wanting desperately to believe this, Wendy put her suspicions aside and attempted to find semblance in her life. My in-laws were also ready to accept this explanation as truth. Sometimes we prefer to avoid the truth because living a lie is easier. I feared that the truth might come back to haunt us.

Soon after, Wendy and Steve's children were being confirmed at the Methodist church they attended. This beautiful sacrament was tainted by a feeling of uneasiness. Wendy made every effort to appear as a happy wife and proud mother. For the sake of her children, she didn't let hostility enter the church. Oh how I wish this was not a façade, but I knew better. Often, I had to put up a strong front when inside I was crumbling because of my husband's behavior. Somehow, I felt connected to Wendy.

As time progressed, Steve began to make himself less available to his family. He would blame it on his efforts to find a new job, but Wendy was growing intensely skeptical. They began to fight all the time. Ironically, I once envied their lives. Now I understood how fragile life really was. I prayed that they would not be forced to endure the same hardships my family had gone through. I had fought for my marriage. Wendy's circumstances could prove worse and be beyond saving.

With their marriage falling apart, Wendy was forced to find full-time employment. Like me, she did not have a college background and lacked work experience. Her prior job as a substitute teacher was not guaranteed work, and she needed a steady income. Steve had found employment as a manager at a convenience store. His income would not support two households. My father-in-law was generous enough to help Wendy find a house to rent for her and the children. With the help of a friend, she soon found a full-time job. Persistency paid off! While our suffering cannot compare to Wendy's, Steve hurt our family. The sadness in my husband's eyes was evident. I was praying that he would not turn to the bottle to ease his sorrow. I was relieved that Wendy's life was becoming more stable, now that her divorce was final. Raising two children as a single mom can prove quite taxing. I prayed Steve's decisions would not have long-lasting negative effects on his family, especially the children. Sincerely, they were the innocent victims without a voice.

For twelve years, I was blessed to have my sister Suzanne and her family living a mile from my house. I relied on my sister so many times when Frank was drinking. I'm sure I drove her crazy with my insecurities and codependence, but she still remained my loyal friend. I had so few friends and was depressed when Suzanne told me that they were relocating to Ohio. Her husband was being transferred, so basically they didn't have a choice. Oh, how I missed them. Selfishly, I wanted and needed them to stay. With my life still unbalanced, I benefited from the unconditional love a sister offered. Sure, I still was able to telephone her, but seeing her in person was irreplaceable.

After fifteen years of living in our house, it started to show its age. We contemplated moving and purchasing a new home but changed our minds. Instead, we chose to renovate our existing house. We loved the neighborhood and our pool in the back. Most of the new construction we toured had a postage stamp for a yard. Frank would be taking the kids to Myrtle Beach while I remained home. Seeming like a good idea, our separation could have positive ramifications. Frank could assume the leadership role with the children, while spending time with his cousins. I needed to trust him and deserved some alone time. I looked forward to overseeing the remodeling of our home. I would be able to focus without worrying about dinners and laundry. However, a call from my daughter Maryanne forced me to second-guess this decision. She voiced her suspicions about her father's drinking. Apparently, Frank had gone over to my parent's home and cried when he shared the story about his brother Steve. Sure, Frank could be sensitive, but this was a little odd. To add more skepticism, Frank's mom told me that a longtime friend of theirs was questioning his behavior. His actions were peculiar, and she described him as being different. That was when the red flag was raised. I hoped that this was untrue. I dreaded my family's return, not because I didn't miss them, but because I wanted to avoid seeing Frank. Perhaps my dream would come to an end. When Frank returned, he fully denied the accusations. His response was instead, "I'll prove to you that I'm not drinking!" Actions speak louder than words, and I would have to wait for the truth. My sister's words were ringing in my ears. She often reminded me that alcoholics fall off the wagon while in recovery. "Okay, Frank," I pleaded, "it's time to jump back on!"

8

My family returned from vacation while the renovations on the house were nearly completed. Back to the routine of everyday life, Frank was now under my watchful eye. I was happy that the contractors finished their work within the promised timetable. So often you hear horror stories about construction disasters. I had to focus my attention on my husband to keep him from going awry. I didn't have time to worry about much else. To keep things on an even keel, Frank returned to his job, and I handled the responsibilities at home. However, I was eager to explore the possibilities of a new hobby. Returning to work at my sister-in-law's, she persuaded me to sign up for photography classes. Recognizing my passion for clicking pictures, she knew I would enjoy learning more about proper techniques. She was right! The instructor was very knowledgeable, and I left with a better understanding of how to use a camera effectively.

Much to my dismay, Frank would not come clean at work and admit to others that he had stopped drinking. For some reason, he didn't want them to know. Perhaps in his eyes, this was a sign of weakness. Trying to stay positive, I wanted to believe him. If they knew he wasn't drinking, then they would not expect to see him consume alcohol. If they didn't know, then drinking would not be an issue. Weighing on my mind, this uncertainty plagued me whenever Frank was at work. I knew I could not confront his family. This would only anger Frank. His family was very private, a trait that Frank had acquired. Our business should be kept behind closed doors.

Our children had grown, and changes to our house were inevitable. In years past, the living room served as their playroom. Now, they no longer required this space and chose instead to reside in their own private bedrooms. I now could take back my living room and make it more grown up. A fresh coat of paint would liven up the room for little cost. Hiring a painter would increase the expense; therefore, I chose to do it myself. Looking back, I may have changed this decision. Upon finishing the job, I was overcome with back pain. Every time I stood, excruciating jolts ran from my back down my right leg. Consulting a doctor, I was informed that an MRI was necessary to determine the cause. I was not privy to the details of a MRI and did not like what I discovered. Lying completely still in a closed capsule for twenty minutes was not appealing to someone who suffers from claustrophobia. Bravely, I went ahead and scheduled an appointment. I would have the procedure at midnight. Apparently, there were so many that required this service, and they ran throughout the night. Too quickly, the evening arrived, and I was prepared to leave. Unfortunately, Frank was not. Recently I had begun sleeping in my daughter's room because Frank and I had a waterbed. The lack of support offered only added to my discomfort, so for now I had to resort to new sleeping quarters. The clock was ticking, and I knew I had to leave without Frank. Used to broken promises, I was resolved to; once again, ignore my husband's self-serving attitude. My mind screamed, *Why bother?*

Arriving on time and alone, I was directed to a room and placed within the confines of an apparatus that was haunting but necessary. Sliding into the closed tunnel, I could hardly contain my beating heart. Firmly closing my eyes, I looked to others for support. Praying the "Our Father" and pleading to my aunt who had passed away, I asked for their comfort. Experiencing the longest twenty minutes of my life, this could not end quickly enough. I tried to remain thankful. Compared to those less fortunate, I was not burdened with health issues that required frequent visits to hospitals. There was always someone else worse off, and I was keenly aware how blessed I truly was. The results were not life threatening. Apparently, I was suffering from a herniated disk. With conditioning and exercise, I would strengthen my back and lessen the chance of reoccurrence. Frank wanted my company back in our bedroom and ordered a new mattress to appease me. We chose a Sleep Number mattress that allows you to choose the level of support. What a difference this made for my ailing back.

Frank had to leave on a business trip to Ohio. Usually, he would drive to his accounts and spend a few nights away from home. At times, he would ride with either his brother or his father. This particular trip, he went alone. Driving home, Frank lost control of the Expedition and landed upside down in a ditch. I was in shock when I received a call from the state police. I was relieved that Frank was unharmed but alarmed when I was informed that he was arrested for a DUI. Calling from jail, he denied the officer's accusations and stated that he was innocent. He seemed to be doing well and now had let this happen. Not realizing the seriousness of his disease, I thought he could easily make the right choice. Basically, you either drink or you don't. I did not contemplate nor place any emphasis on need or dependence. I figured Frank drank because he wanted to, not because he had to. Due to this ignorance, I was mad and unsympathetic to his setbacks.

In an attempt to down play the significance of a DUI, Frank was complacent and accepted the court's decision. He would have to complete community service and take part in AA classes as a form of punishment. Routinely, he would also have to visit his probation officer, who would document and monitor his progress. Ironically, I envisioned my husband sitting before my father not as a son-in-law, but as a parolee. On one of his visits, Frank was asked to submit to a breathalyzer. His probation officer had reason to believe that he had consumed alcohol. Perhaps Frank was exhibiting odd behavior, or the smell on his breath was pervasive. Regardless, the results were conclusive. Hauled back to jail a second time, my husband sought to blame others. As a kid, he would blame others for his bad behavior, and as an adult, he found other scapegoats. Most of the time, I fell victim to his blame. It was almost like I was opening his mouth and pouring the liquid down his throat. This may sound absurd to most, but for Frank it was his reality.

Quite frustrated, I began going to Al-Anon again. I was hoping they could help me understand what was happening. Handling a situation that I could not control was difficult. I hoped that my decision to stay with Frank was right. I knew that my children were my utmost priority, and I hoped that my decision to stay would not harm them. Teaching CCD and attending church was a source of strength that I sought and gained weekly. Listening to the homily, the priest would share his opinions about life and establish that no one said it would be easy. I knew then that I belonged in church and needed to hear those words. For me, life was not easy, at least not right now. But I also believed that somehow I would become stronger and better because I didn't give up. Trying to live my life like an Al-Anon member, I strove to separate my world from living with an alcoholic. This world was positive, happy, and thankful. This was the side of me that I wanted others to see and experience. In a sense, I was embarrassed to let people know that my life was quite different. Insanely, we are so obsessed with what others think. Perhaps I would have been given more respect if they knew the obstacles I was facing while maintaining my dignity and pride.

Due to Frank's repeated offenses, he was not permitted to drink in front of me and the kids. Sadly, he was still drinking and hiding bottles of vodka around the house. Continually, I would listen as he swore to his sobriety and reassured me that he was fine. Frank's office was only fifteen minutes from the house, yet I worried about him driving home daily. I knew he was drinking, and I feared that he would lose control of his vehicle. Also, I was troubled with the idea of him losing his job. What would happen if his bosses discovered his problem and were able to recognize that he was often drunk on the job?

Maryanne would soon be attending college, and knowing this made me stronger in my conviction to keep Frank sober. If I left him, he might spiral down even more. Financially, this could devastate our family, and my children and I would suffer the consequences. Maryanne deserved the opportunity to further her education, and I felt responsible as a parent to assist her in this quest. I did make one demand of Frank. He was still spending time with a neighbor who once lived near us. Already, he had been divorced twice and was living a life that I simply abhorred. He was a heavy drinker who loved to spend time in strip joints. Appearing almost jealous of our lives, he wanted Frank's company and attempted to make him part of his lifestyle. You know what they say, "Misery loves company." I gave Frank an ultimatum. He must choose either him or me. Thankfully, this man became a part of our history.

Out of the blue, Frank received a very generous perk from work. His employer was sponsoring a trip to Rome, Italy, and Frank was being considered to attend. For me, this would be a dream come true. Being Roman Catholic, I would relish the idea of visiting a country with which I shared religious ties. My in-laws offered to babysit while we were away. Anxious with anticipation, I awaited the news hopeful that Frank was chosen. Within two weeks, a decision had been made. Frank and I were going to Italy! I was on top of the world, and nothing could spoil this glorious mood, or so I thought.

This year, the kids and I would be going to Myrtle Beach without Frank. He would be left to care for our pets, a job I take very seriously. Frank would work out of our house. His employer would soon be shutting down his office anyway to save money. I felt happy knowing that the animals would have supervision throughout most of the day. Surely, Frank would behave responsibly. Within a couple of days, I began to doubt my husband's accountability. His voice was slurred when he spoke, and his attitude was quite ornery. Finding it hard to enjoy the rest of our vacation, I tried my best to hide my displeasure from the kids and my family. I prayed for the safety of our animals. How dare Frank put me in this predicament.

Arriving home, furious, I confronted Frank. Unfortunately, my efforts were proving to be fruitless. Deep down, Frank knew I would forgive him. Why should he bother to change? Frank's ego, coupled with my love, gave him the confidence to continue drinking. He never physically abused me, and he was too ignorant to realize that verbal abuse was just as damaging. I often wondered if I would have left if he hit me. We often separate physical abuse from verbal and underrate the effects of the latter. Continuing to read the literature from Al-Anon, I prayed that Frank would change and overcome his demon, the bottle.

As our trip to Rome approached, my feeling of eagerness was replaced with thoughts of uncertainty because the fights between Frank and me continued No matter how many times I try to convince Frank that I would not go to Rome, he refused to stop drinking. To make matters worse, I injured my ankle while taking my dog for a walk. Crying out in pain, I begged Maryanne to get the car. Luckily she had accompanied me in my walk that day. I was unable to finish our walk. I hoped that my trip would not be ruined. Frank had already dampened my expectations, now I had to contend with this. We were scheduled to leave the following day, regardless of my hesitation.

Arriving at the airport, it felt surreal. Never in a million years did I ever expect to be traveling to Italy. Icing my ankle before we left, I was determined to keep the swelling down. I had received a new camera for Mother's Day and was excited to break it in. Overall, I had great expectations for this trip with Frank. On the ride to the airport, we openly discussed my disapproval for his drinking. Hopefully, the ten days we spent together would alleviate any temptation. In my company, Frank would not have the opportunity to drink because rest assured, there wouldn't be alcohol in my presence.

The plane ride over the Atlantic Ocean was a bit scary and made me a little uncomfortable. My throbbing ankle was a constant reminder for the pain I had endured, but I knew it would all be worth it. When the plane touched down, my body was pumped with adrenaline. I would need this energy to make up for the time difference my body would soon experience. Setting our watches six hours ahead, we would have to adjust to Italy's time zone. Chartered busses and tour guides were at the airport ready to greet us and take us to the hotel. I was overwhelmed to see our beautiful accommodations. Feeling like royalty, I was so thankful to be afforded such luxury. I immediately iced my ankle to prepare for the tours the next day. I would not be slowed down because of this injury. I knew I might never get this chance again and did not want to miss one sight.

Our sightseeing began at the Colosseum. This magnificent building was still three fourths intact after 2,000 years. Then we viewed the beautiful Basilica. There were not words to describe the extraordinary paintings and intricate statues. Astounded, I stared in disbelief at the workmanship these artists portrayed. Our next stop was at the Vatican. I was humbled to stand before such a blessed place and felt at peace among members so holy. Working up my hunger, I was looking forward to enjoying a meal with two other couples that we had befriended. To think, all our meals were included. The only drawback to this dining experience was the complimentary bottle of wine served at each meal besides breakfast. The Italians sure do enjoy their vintage products. I was waiting for Frank to tell our friends that he didn't drink, but these words never came. Well, I would not let it get the better of me. Our friends were probably left wondering why we never shared a glass, but I watched as they enjoyed theirs.

The next day, we spent our time in Florence. Walking around this picturesque city, we admired the churches, statues, and fountains that seemed to grace every corner. I enjoyed the shops and kiosks that lined the streets. They specialized in jewelry. Searching for a unique gift for each daughter, I found a piece of jewelry to suit their individual tastes.

Pompeii was one of the most educational cities we visited. After the eruption of Vesuvius in AD 79, it was a miracle that this city was preserved and not destroyed. I was able to appreciate the life of Romans through the artifacts they left behind. The people of Italy should be proud of their abilities to preserve their culture and not replace it with modern technologies. Too often, we are quick to destroy buildings and such that represent our history. It may force me to think twice now before I get rid of things I once considered old and worthless. The next morning, we toured the city of Rome. With so much to see, I could go on forever describing all the elements this city offered. I never knew so many ruins, fountains, and churches existed. I went through eight rolls of film photographing what we saw and hoping to preserve the memories. That evening, I decided to take my camera out and click pictures of Rome at night. They came out amazing.

Sadly, our trip was nearing the end. Thankful that Frank had his drinking under control, I was confident that our last couple of days would end on a positive note. Jumping on a tour bus, we maneuvered up the coast of the Mediterranean. Feeling like the bus could suddenly veer off the road; I was relieved once we arrived in the city of Sorrento. After lunch, Frank and I decided to purchase a handmade jewelry box for each of the girls. Having more patience, I waited while they carefully boxed each one. Meanwhile, Frank decided to meet up with his male cohorts. Departing the store, I was unaware of Frank's whereabouts but quickly found him. Apparently, the men had asked him to join them in a drink. Famous for the Lemon Cello, Sorrento boasted this flavorful drink, and my husband's curiosity was peaked. I looked down and observed Frank's empty glass in distaste. I overhead one of his friends remark, "You are supposed to sip not gulp, this cocktail." Obviously, they were not privy to Frank's ploy to outwit me. Yelling throughout the streets of Sorrento, I made quite a scene. Unfortunately, our new friends were seeing a darker, less appealing side of me. I wish I could have contained my emotions but found it impossible. Frank attempted to soothe my anger by purchasing a bottle of this liquor for his father. Right then, he failed to appease me. Overall, our trip was spectacular, but Frank's last episode would linger for quite some time, along with the jet lag.

9

Returning home and dealing with reality was difficult. Unfortunately, Frank's drinking was escalating, and it did not appear to be getting any better. Vodka bottles were jammed into his golf bag. He was creating all sorts of hiding places. When I confronted him, he would respond by turning the tables and placing the blame on me. I had the problem, not him. Continuing to put me down, Frank resorted to name calling; and the titles he chose were not very complimentary. Sadly, my children overheard many of our heated arguments. Reminding them that their father's ridiculing was inappropriate, I hoped I could convince them that this was unacceptable. Trying to focus on myself, I decided to purchase tickets to see Fleetwood Mac. My best friend also enjoyed this group, and we planned on going together. Looking forward to a girl's night out, I was disappointed that Frank did not feel the same way. Whenever I tried to be independent, Frank would become hostile. I do not believe he wanted me to make any decisions on my own. Ignoring his contradictory attitude, I was hell-bent on going anyway. I truly enjoyed the concert and do not regret my decision. Standing up to

Frank was something I needed to do more often. If only he could be happy for me instead.

On a path of self-destruction, Frank was out of control. He did not make any attempt to stop drinking and showed absolutely no remorse. I knew that I did not have any other alternative and contacted a divorce attorney. Making my phone call obvious to Frank, I hoped this would trigger some type of emotion. Perhaps he would feel my loss was too much to risk and put down the bottle. This was wishful thinking on my part. The lawyer required a $2,500 retainer fee. He also suggested that I open my own checking account. If not, I could be left penniless. I would not put it past Frank to wipe out our accounts. People can be very spiteful when seeking revenge. Wisely, I took his advice and immediately left for the bank. Upon returning, I found Frank asleep on the recliner. This was a typical daily event for him; but today I needed to wake him to discuss my transactions. Anger was not vivid enough to describe his reaction. Vulgar four-letter words spewed out of his mouth. He described lawyers in unkindly terms and did not have much better to say about me. Evidently Frank had no intention of changing regardless of what I said or did.

During this time, I was working part-time at a photography studio at Target and also doing some substitute teaching. I found it impossible to remain fully focused on my jobs but gave it my best effort. Realistically speaking, I would need to add experience to my resume if I wanted to attain full-time employment. Scared, I sought the support of family and friends. Everyone, including Frank's parents, was sympathetic and available to lean on. I informed the lawyer about Frank's abuse, and he said that our next step was to remove him from the house. In an attempt to make it legal, I visited our local courthouse. Unfortunately, I did not have legal recourse. I was told that Frank's verbal abuse was not sufficient enough to demand he leave. Rather, if physical abuse had taken place, then my pleas would have been taken seriously. I knew Frank would not leave willingly. I went ahead with the formalities and my lawyer drew up the divorce papers. Ironically, less than a month before, I was enjoying the trip of a lifetime in Italy, a pleasure few get to experience. Now, I was fearful of my future, both financially and emotionally. Crazily, I still counted my blessings.

Within a couple of days, Frank had an awakening. Both the children and I were ready for a change, with or without him. Thankfully, they had my back. Without the kids' acceptance, I probably would have backed down. Almost immediately, Frank's demeanor began to change. I watched as he went from being cocky to showing signs of humbleness. Begging, Frank promised to sign himself into rehab if I would call the lawyer and withdraw the papers. Oh, how I wanted to believe him. Scared for both the children and myself, I considered his apology. My head was filled with so many uncertainties. The kids would be forced to leave their friends and their school if I left. I could never afford to support them in our current home, and I knew Frank would not agree to pay hefty spousal and child support. I feared that his drinking would become worse without us and he would perhaps lose his job. Then what? How would Maryanne go to college, and who would raise my children while I worked two, maybe three, jobs? Praying for Frank's sobriety, I began to ponder the nine months when he didn't drink. That was the life I wanted for me and my children and even Frank. Donning my rose-colored glasses, I placed my faith in Frank's word and made the call to the lawyer. Questioning my decision, he informed me that he would hold on to the papers in case I changed my mind. I got the feeling that my see-saw behavior was common among women contemplating divorce and my case was not unique.

As promised, Frank went to rehab for a weekend to dry out. This turned out to be a feeble attempt to appease me. If Frank was trying to convince me that he was making every effort to change, his actions proved differently. I was tired of hearing Frank's infamous quote, "Let's just start over." However he still continued to belittle and disrespect me. I allowed myself to be manipulated by his empty promises. I knew in my heart that Frank wanted to change; however, his disease made it impossible. I remembered an uncle of Frank's that had died from alcoholism. He was only in his early fifties. I began to question the validity of alcoholism being hereditary. Perhaps Frank's genes had something to do with his need or desire to drink. This knowledge made me more sympathetic to Frank, but I have to admit, I still didn't condone his behavior. I just came to the realization that this battle would be more difficult than I had anticipated. I would have to live with my decision to stay and would hopefully learn from this experience. It would obviously take more than threats to get Frank to stop.

I would often call Frank at his office to check up on him. I was suspicious that he was drinking at work and needed some form of comfort. By hearing his voice, I could assume he was all right and at least not driving around. There were times that Frank would ignore my calls, putting me into panic mode. I continually worried about him arriving home safely and feared his condition if and when he did. Never admitting that he was drunk, I was called nuts. The children were trying to avoid him and the situation by staying away as much as possible. I did not blame them. I found some solace by working, but this also led to anxiousness. It seemed the more I worked, the more Frank drank. Most of the time, I would find him passed out on the recliner when I came home. I was torn between my responsibilities at home which I felt included my pets, children, husband, and my own sense of happiness. During this time of my life, I didn't really know what the definition of happiness was. I was simply living day by day and thanking God for each moment, no matter what the moment was like.

One particular day, I decided to surprise Frank at work after being unable to reach him by telephone. Honestly, I was trying to catch him red-handed. Sick of his denials, I was looking for proof. I was surprised to find Frank sleeping in his car in the parking lot.

Grabbing his keys, I left him there. Too upset to even wake him, I felt revolted and refused to drive him home. I knew this would only lead to more fighting, and I didn't feel like dealing with it. Let him find a way home! Apparently, he wasn't too concerned because he arrived home after nine o'clock. A taxi arrived in my driveway with Frank as the passenger. I listened to him as he tried to persuade the driver to take him to Buckhead. Knowing all too well about this location, I assumed Frank was not ready to call it a night and was tempted by strip joints. Either that, or else he was trying to get back at me. Thankfully, the driver was aware of his condition and left him at the bottom of our driveway. Watching Frank sway back and forth like a top as he walked up the driveway, I felt compelled to laugh. It was either this or cry. Here was this man with a fantastic job and a loving family drunk as a skunk. Evidently he didn't care about himself. Barely making it into the house, he collapsed on the family room rug. I refused to watch him sleep and went over to a neighbor's house. I needed to vent, and I needed a listening ear. She was amazed by my strength and ability to endure this lifestyle. Faith told me I was not alone. Listening to the homilies at church, I would reflect upon the messages. No one said life would be easy. Alcoholism is like cancer. I would not leave my husband if he was dying from cancer. My friends and family would tell me to leave, but I heard another voice asking me to stay. One day, I remember begging God to send me a sign. As I was preparing for my upcoming lesson for CCD, I grabbed my CCD book and was drawn to the middle. I opened to a chapter entitled, "Sacraments of forgiveness and marriage." Was this the sign that I was looking for? Remembering the vows Frank and I took, for better or worse, I believed that the best was yet to come. I knew I still loved Frank and tried to focus on his goodness. If only he would agree to rehab for longer than one weekend. Speaking to my mother-in-law on the phone, we discussed the possibility of persuading Frank to submit to serious long-term help. Knowing that his prior efforts were failures, we both agreed that he was not doing enough. I was so appreciative of my in-laws' support. They had become such an integral part of my life and such a blessing to me and the kids.

My father-in-law had retired, and Frank would soon begin working out of the house. For me, this would be a mixed blessing. I felt reassured because he was not behind the wheel of his car while driving back and forth to his office. Too often, I worried that he was driving under the influence. However, he would be home twenty-four seven, except when away on business. Knowing Frank's personality, I would have to adjust to his constant company, and this would not always be pleasant. At times, he appeared to be a caged lion, pacing to and fro, a bundle of anxious energy. I was still working part-time at both jobs, which offered some relief and deterrence. Frank had his job and colleagues to keep him occupied. I hoped this would keep him out of trouble. His employer was unaware of his condition, and I was confident that he would not jeopardize his position. I could never imagine being so self-indulgent and putting my family at risk. Frank was being so selfish. This uncertainty caused knots in my stomach. Again I was worrying about his job and what would happen to us if he lost it.

This day, Frank decided to work from home. He had some Antibuse left over from rehab and promised to take this pill to prevent him from drinking. If he drank while on this medication, he would become violently ill. I was pleased with his decision and felt comfortable to go on a walk. En route, I ran into my neighbor who was going through a divorce. She was always there for me in times of turmoil, and I felt compelled to reciprocate. I invited her to join Frank and me for lunch. We were planning on going to Chili's, and I was happy to have her as our guest. Without any children, I figured she must be lonely. I was hoping to brighten her day with some companionship. She agreed, and Frank and I picked her up a while later. I was disappointed when we arrived at Chili's. My inquisitive friend asked me, "What's wrong with Frank?" Suddenly,

I began to wonder if this lunch date was a good idea. Afraid to hear her response, I meekly asked, "What do you mean?" Apparently, she could smell alcohol on Frank's breath and wondered if he had broken his promise. Why wasn't the Antibuse doing its job? The appetite I once had was gone. Once again, Frank had effectively ruined a pleasant time. The minute we arrived home, I confronted Frank. He nonchalantly admitted to spitting out the pill. To make matters even worse, he advised me that he wouldn't be taking them again. Frank's chance for recovery began to look bleaker. I questioned whether or not pills, threats, or intervention would make any difference. Frank needed to take control. He needed to want to stop, and he needed to do it for himself. As life went on, I would still try to fix Frank's problem, still not quite getting that it was not my problem to fix. Until Frank looked his demon in the face, nothing I could do or say would make him better.

Soon after, Frank surprised his mother and me with a phone call on the way to work. He had made the choice to check himself into rehab, and more importantly, he felt resolved to do it alone. We were so excited. Finally, he was coming to his senses. A couple of hours passed, and I tried calling Frank. I was eager to hear about his progress and find out how long he would be staying. By late afternoon, I had still not heard from him and was beginning to worry. To alleviate my concern, I decided to drive by the center to see for myself. Arriving to the parking lot, I swore I saw Frank leaving. How could that be? He sounded so sure of his decision. Deciding it must have been someone else, I drove through the entire lot searching for his car. After two attempts, I concluded that his vehicle was not here. Apparently, my eyes were not deceiving me, and that was Frank leaving. Trying to stay calm, I called my girlfriend. Right now, I needed more than Christian music to sooth my nerves. Jumping on the interstate to drive home, I began to approach the scene of an accident. I feared that it was Frank. My friend stayed on the phone with me, attempting to soothe my concerns until I came upon the collision. Thankfully, Frank's car was not involved. Relieved, I became angrier at Frank. I thought to myself, *How many times would he risk endangering himself and innocent others?* I felt like his luck would eventually run out. I did not believe he had the right to back down. He should have gone to rehab, and he should have stayed. What right did he have to give us all false hope? How dare he disappoint me and his family! He simply stated, "I changed my mind." I did not know how to respond, so I yelled and we fought. That much had not changed.

10

The only reprieve from Frank's drinking was during the holidays. During these occasions, he would abstain from alcohol, which saved him and my family from embarrassment. Seeing that he could become quite ornery when drunk, I was thankful that my family did not have to witness this behavior. For me, Christmas was a time of giving and nothing made me happier than watching loved ones open presents. I did not want these memories to be spoiled by Frank's antics. My parents would spend every other Christmas with us. Because my time with them was limited, I wanted every minute to be special. It seemed that the moment they left, Frank would go downhill and return to the bottle. It appeared that he was rewarding himself for being on his best behavior. Just another excuse to add to his repertoire, Frank was trying to justify his actions. For now, my parents were saved from seeing their son-in-law's struggle. I guess I was relieved that they didn't have to worry about me and their grandchildren. They would be sickened if they knew the truth.

I discovered one of Frank's favorite hiding places to store his empty bottles. He discarded the empty bottles above the air conditioning vents in the garage. Like most days, I was suspicious that

Frank was intoxicated and went to investigate. Against my better judgment, I was snooping while he was sleeping. The counselors at Al-Anon did not recommend this action. They suggested that if the perpetrator was confronted with evidence, he or she would only purchase more. Anger and accusations would only fuel the fire within the alcoholic. Contrary to this knowledge, I couldn't fight off the temptation. I hoped and prayed that if I found the evidence, Frank would finally admit that he needed help. I uncovered a fancy liquor bottle during this particular search. For some reason, this expensive bottle caused me to see a darker shade of red. Furious, I bolted up the stairs, bottle in hand. Now Frank was not only drinking, he thought he deserved top shelf. The nerve of him! Yelling, I confronted Frank with this heavy glass bottle. Taking a swing, I brandished the bottle in front of him, aiming at his arm. POP! The sound of the glass hitting Frank was louder than I expected. This was not Frank's ordinary plastic bottle. Unfortunately, this weapon was much more damaging. To heighten the severity of my attack, my aim was off and the blow landed on Frank's chin. Immediately, I felt a sense of remorse and shame. I saw the trail of blood lead from his chin onto his shirt. My irrational behavior had caused injury, and for this I was deeply ashamed. Knowing I could not take it back, I had to deal with the consequences. Frank began screaming obscenities at me. In a way, I did not blame him. However, his fury seemed to escalate as the minutes ticked slowly by. I wished this nightmare would end. I had no other alternative and was forced to call Frank's parents. Perhaps their arrival would trigger Frank to become submissive. In my company alone, this was not happening. Within thirty long minutes, they arrived, and finally I was able to let out a sigh of relief. Maybe they could talk some sense into their son.

Taking my side, they tried to lessen the seriousness of Frank's cut. They too were fed up with his drinking and would not make me look like the villain. I had once again gone against the teach-

DEROUIN & DIROCCO

88

ings of Al-Anon and involved others. They tried to persuade me to separate my life from the alcohol, but I found this impossible. My Italian temper got the best of me, and I reacted without thinking. When the atmosphere finally calmed, my in-laws left. I continued to reassure Frank that his injury was not substantial and he would be okay. Listening, he laid it to rest, and I was able to find some peace. Trying to put this behind would prove difficult. Whenever I looked at Frank, the scar under his chin would serve as a reminder. Sure, Frank needed to change, but I too would have to reflect upon my choices.

My volunteering for Meals on Wheels had come to an end. They no longer required my services. I did continue teaching CCD. I was glad to have an outlet to get away from Frank, but I cannot say that I didn't worry every minute. I knew that when I was away from home, Frank would take advantage of my absence and drink. To think, I was out trying to help others while he selfishly only thought of himself. Whenever I confronted him, fights would ensue. Surely my neighbors must have heard our screaming matches. How embarrassing! I was not the culprit, yet I was part of the havoc. Once again I had made the choice to involve myself in Frank's world. It was time that I learned to separate myself from him. I'm not referring to divorce, but I would need to allow him to stand alone and face the consequences if he drank. I would be there for him if and when he asked for it. Until then, there was nothing I could do.

Summer arrived, and it was time to prepare another trip to Myrtle Beach for the kids and me. I was tossed between regretting that Frank was staying behind and grateful that I would not be worried if he came. In the perfect world, I would love to have my husband join on this family trip; however, my reality would prevent this from happening. Our past vacations were ruined by his drinking, and I was tired of being embarrassed. I cherished these trips to the beach, spending time with my sisters and watching the cousins bond. Luckily, my children and I have fond memories; unfortunately, Frank does not. As usual, he promised to stay sober while we were away. Unable to trust his word, I highly doubted that he would live up to this promise. I suppose you can only cry wolf so many times until people stop believing you.

When we returned from the beach this year, I was anxious for my daughter Maryanne. She would be starting college at UGA that fall. I was so very proud of her accomplishments, and I knew Frank was too. Living away from home, Maryanne would forge her independence and establish herself as a woman. Unlike myself, I wanted her to pursue her education and gain financial freedom as an adult. It would be difficult for me to prove myself independently because I had forgone my education and chosen to get married and begin a family. While I am thankful for my blessings, I do realize that I limited my career choices because of this decision. During our frequent trips to Maryanne's dorm, Frank appeared to be sober. I was glad for my daughter's sake. I knew she was nervous and eager to begin this new life and didn't need to worry about her father. Ironically, this time in my life which appeared to be happy also caused friction between my best friend and me. Planning to visit Maryanne, I asked my best friend to accompany me. Never quite knowing Frank's condition, I couldn't rely on him. At the last minute, he decided to come, and I told my friend that I would be going with him instead. She was not pleased with my decision and had a few unkindly words to share. Apparently, she was sick of seeing her friend be twisted by a man who was so inconsistent as a husband and father. Unfortunately, rather than console, she chose to reprimand me. God knows, I had enough of being told what to do and when to do it. I realized that she was looking out for my best interests, but I could not take the nagging and lashed back at her. This led to a confrontation and, for then, ended our friendship. With time, I hoped we would rekindle our relationship. At that point our differences of opinion were too much to handle, but hopefully we would humble ourselves and once again see eye to eye, or at least meet half way.

Soon after, Frank began sleeping on the sofa. Most would not be alarmed by such an event, but instinctively, I knew this meant he was drinking. He was sleeping most of the day, which was odd because I knew he was not ill. In the past, I observed him doing the same and was privy to his routine. Upon waking, Frank would head out the door, and I imagined he drove to the liquor store. While I did not actually know this to be fact, his demeanor was enough to make my suspicions valid. On this particular occasion, I decided to alter his pattern. Carefully reaching into his pocket, I tried not to rouse him from his slumber. My intention was to take his keys and prevent him from leaving. However, I was unsuccessful, and Frank woke up. Furious, he demanded that I give him back his keys. Unwilling to reciprocate, I attempted to get away from his flailing arms. Our dispute turned into a game of cat and mouse. I was the mouse that held the bait, and Frank was the cat determined to get it. Poor Marissa witnessed our escapades. She watched as her father chased her mother out the door and throughout the backyard. I tried to escape into the garage, but Frank was right behind me. Picking up a plastic bottle, he threw it directly for me. Ducking, I turned and came face-to-face with Marissa. How dare he behave violently toward me in front of our daughter. I had no other alternative and called 9–1-1. Determined, I hoped they would force him to get professional help. Frank had another solution, which included his escape. He did not intend to listen to a stranger's advice and was not ready to face the consequences of his abusive actions. Quickly, he dashed out of the garage and into the woods that surround our backyard. With the police on the way, he was not willing to stay around and face the authorities. Firstly, he was obviously intoxicated, and secondly, he already had a DUI record.

When the officers arrived, I felt compelled to press charges. I wanted Marissa to understand the severity of her father's actions and set precedence. No one should be subjected to abuse, and if it does occur, the abuser needs to be punished. Sure, I had second thoughts about having my husband arrested, but he deserved it. He initiated this by choosing to drink and attempting to drive while under the influence. Rather than admitting to his wrongdoing, he wanted to blame me. I started this by stealing his keys. Yeah, right. With a warrant for his arrest, Frank had no choice but to come back and face what he had done.

Once the police left, I called my youngest sister for support. My stomach was in knots, and I knew she would help to calm me. I was worried about Frank's well-being and second-guessing my decision. Reassuring me, my sister confirmed my actions and was confident that he would be home soon. He had left with only the shirt on his back. The fall evenings were cold, and without any money, he would be forced to stay outside. What would he eat and drink? How would he stay warm? Never in a million years did I expect it to come to this. My husband was so successful in the business world but unsuccessful in dealing with everyday life. Seeing that it was Friday, Frank would not have to work the next couple of days, and his employer wouldn't have any recollection of what had transpired. I feared that they would discover his alcoholism and fire him. For now, he was able to keep up the façade, but eventually his transgressions could be discovered.

Soon the night turned into morning, and Frank was still missing. Working on nervous energy, I did my best to keep busy. I talked to my in-laws and family throughout the day, but even they couldn't completely unnerve me. I found it nearly impossible to fall asleep that evening but knew I needed rest in order to stay strong. This was a true test of my faith. Praying, I asked God to keep Frank safe. We still needed him in our lives, and I wanted nothing more than to see him, regardless of his condition. Sure, I was angry, but my love for him was still strong, and I knew that together with the help of God we could overcome his dependence. My prayers were answered, and he stumbled through the door Sunday morning. Tired and unkempt, Frank was a sight for sore eyes. Furious, he insisted that he stayed at a nearby hotel, but from the looks of him, I highly doubted this. I was so thankful that he was unharmed and tried to overlook his physical appearance. I knew I had not done anything wrong, yet I wished he felt the same. He felt I had provoked the situation by stealing his keys. If I had left him alone, he would not have to turn himself into the police for an arrest that he believed was unwarranted. In fact, Frank was breaking the law by returning home and being near his family. Even though I did not feel threatened, he would not be allowed in our presence until he faced the authorities. He needed to accept responsibility and listen while the legal system doled out his punishment. He was given probation and would have to take part in weekly anger management classes. On those Saturdays, Frank would be edgy and impatient. He was convinced that the class was a waste of time, and I had issues, not him. He felt that he was paying for the crimes of everyone else and he was an innocent victim. Continuing to drink behind my back, Frank did not feel any remorse. He was oblivious to any wrong-doing.

I knew better and would have to stand by my conviction. Talking to the kids, I tried to be open and honest about their father's disease. I wanted them to understand that their mother was not mean and vengeful, but that their father needed help. He needed to take the initiative, but in the meantime, I was not going to permit him to hurt us or anyone else. If I needed to take his keys again, I would. Frank was still traveling on business, and sadly, I looked forward to the break. His colleagues believed he would just enjoy cocktails, and they didn't seem concerned about his performance. I would never jeopardize his job by telling them, knowing we could lose everything if I did. Evidently his sales abilities were not affected; therefore, I didn't feel it was necessary to bring it to their attention. If and when it did, they could handle it. In the meantime, I was dealing with keeping my family together and financially afloat. This may have included some deception on my part, but I didn't feel obligated to share Frank's story with everyone. For now, the people I loved and trusted knew the truth, and that was enough for me.

With so many vivid memories, their were some that stood out and lasted more than others. For example, I remember the day that Frank drove up the driveway, quite inebriated. Seeing that he was on probation, Frank was overstepping his boundaries and had no regard for the law. For some reason, he felt above it. Angry, I decided to call my father. I was hoping his experience as a probation officer could shed some light on the situation. I was open to his suggestions and was hoping he could convince Frank to view his offenses as serious. He phoned Frank's probation officer, hoping that he could help. Unfortunately, this plan backfired. By this time, Frank had sobered up and was able to have a conversation that sounded quite logical. He was able to convince his probation officer that I was imagining things and he was never drunk. My emotions were getting the best of me. I had nothing to worry about. He was fine. Hanging up the phone, Frank had once again eluded the truth. However, I knew I wasn't crazy and was convinced he was still drinking. He might be able to trick some, but he wasn't able to fool me. Once the classes were finished, Frank would be off probation. Evidently he had not changed and had learned nothing from this experience. An unwilling student, he would not admit to anger issues, nor make any attempt to accept responsibility for his drinking. Still I continued to pray and ask for God's intervention. Perhaps this was part of his plan to make me stronger in my faith. Willing to accept his help, I was not ready to give up on Frank.

11

Feeling very lonely, I missed talking to my best friend. I could not blame her. My indecision was quite exhausting, and I'm sure she grew tired of hearing, "I am telling Frank I want a divorce, and then I am giving him another chance." Inside, she was probably scream- ing, "Make up your mind!" I too was growing weary of listening to my own conscience. They say that friends come and go, but I knew in my heart our friendship would endure this setback. For now, I would have to deal with Frank's antics alone, without her advice. So in turn, I cried on the shoulders of my sisters and in-law, hoping family would have more patience.

Frank continued to do stupid and thoughtless things. One day, he had left to go out of town. Calling from the airplane, he asked that I drive to the airport immediately. Apparently, he had mis- placed his wallet and was concerned that it had dropped outside his vehicle in the parking lot. Feeling put out, I was angry that I would have to make the fifty minute drive to the airport in traffic, due to Frank's irresponsibility. Pulling out of the garage, my car became the target of two falling vodka bottles. Once again, Frank had hidden his empty bottles on top of the air conditioning vents. I was trying to do him a favor. Instead of being told thank you, I felt like Frank had slapped me in the face. The only good outcome was finding his wallet on the floorboard of his car. With relief, I drove home, happy that Frank would be far away and would not be home to face my wrath. Unnerved by my threats, he was oblivious to my yelling anyway.

Using Marissa as a decoy, Frank decided to go behind my back again and purchase a new puppy. Unaware of his motives, I knew he was up to something. It was not commonplace for him to take his daughters for a drive, usually he did this alone. Returning from the pet store, Marissa had an adorable Pekingese puppy wrapped in her arms. How could I be angry when my daughter was so happy? Frank had done it again. He knew that I would be sympathetic to my daughters, and he also knew how much I loved animals. Using this as ammunition, he did what he thought was best. In his warped mind, he believed that a new pet would bring much needed joy into our home. What he failed to recognize was that a new puppy would only add more stress to my life. There were so many issues to consider, and Frank had not used logic when making this rash decision. We already had a nine and a half year old Lab who had just recently lost his best friend (our twelve and a half year old female Shar-Pei). He did not give us any time to mourn and love on just him for awhile. Now, my big boy would have to take a back seat to this puppy. This was not fair at all! Also, I would be responsible for training and caring for this puppy. I did not ask for this extra responsibility and felt I already had enough on my plate. Working as a substitute teacher and employed as a photographer part-time, work coupled with household duties was overwhelming. Plus, Frank's condition had not improved. I was tired of watching him sleep while I ran the house. I must admit that my daughters and I learned how to tiptoe quietly around Frank while he slept. Most of the time, we preferred to deal with him sleeping rather than living with him awake. Finding that my time was being stretched too thin, I quit my photography job and focused on teaching. This was a better fit for the kids and me, seeing that Frank was not part of the equation.

Putting my life in perspective, I realized times with Frank were difficult, but this paled in comparison to some people's suffering. Watching the news, I observed that things could be much worse, as it was for many. Recently, my sister-in-law's good friend from high school was diagnosed with skin cancer. With only a few months to live, she was facing the reality of death. Divorced and raising two beautiful daughters, she had to accept the realization that she may have to leave her family behind. She was only forty-two years old, much too young to contemplate dying. She had so much to live for but wasn't given the opportunity to explore her future. Unfortunately, she succumbed to this disease, having given the fight of her life. I too was determined to fight. While my struggle was quite different, I knew Frank was lucky. His disease was not yet terminal, and I would make every effort to help him survive. Perhaps my fate was to be married to him, for God knew that I would have the strength and faith to stay by his side.

The media did not help support my battle. Every day, I had to watch people on television drinking and partying. Quite frankly, Americans are notorious for glorifying alcohol. Sure, they remind you to drink responsibly, but I did not feel this was a legitimate warning. I do agree that a casual cocktail is okay, but for people like Frank, this is not possible. He was not capable of drinking responsibly, and I wished he was not tempted by outside sources. I could control myself and not drink in front of him, but I was not able to stop him from watching television and hanging out with friends who drink. I realize we grow from avoiding temptation and have to acquire this skill on our own, but I wish things could have been a little bit easier. Cigarette ads are banned from television, yet alcohol is not. In my opinion, both are lethal.

Trying not to let my worries about Frank consume my life, I would leave for work positive. I truly loved working with kids and was thankful to have such a wonderful and rewarding career. My morning progressed quite smoothly. Calling Frank whenever I got a break, I was satisfied that he was sober and fulfilling his duties for work. By one, my concerns rose. Now my calls would go unanswered. Suddenly, my sunny personality grew ominous, and I found that time ticked slowly by. Finding it impossible to focus, I tried my best to finish the day without letting it affect my work performance. I was anxious to return home, afraid of where or how I would find Frank. Most likely he was drunk. But I could never tell how drunk. My biggest fear was finding him dead. Wanting nothing more than to be nonchalant, I could not help caring about Frank, even after all that he had done. They say that love is blind. For me, I was hoping and praying to see the real Frank. I knew deep within was a man who wanted to be a good husband and father. In the past, Frank had been fun loving and generous. Oh, how I wished we could turn back the clock and remove the evils of alcoholism.

Frank knew exactly what buttons to push when it came to the kids. He would often suggest that we get another Pekingese puppy, and of course, they agreed. I would become obstinate, refusing to go along with their wishes. Taking Frank's side, the girls would beg and plead with me to change my mind. Ironically, this was one of the few times I saw Frank and the kids in unison. Most of the time, they went their separate ways. Perhaps the children were avoiding him and most often he was too drunk to notice. I decided against my better judgment to buy the puppy on my own. For once, I wanted it to be my choice, not Frank's. I figured I might as well beat him to the punch. I chose a beautiful female Pekingese puppy. My poor Lab now had two puppies to contend with. A trooper, he tolerated the feisty puppies and never showed any domination. I continued to walk him almost every day. We were like two peas in a pod. Our lives were not exactly like we wanted them to be. We dealt with the adversity and tried to make the best of a bad situation. Walking side by side, we rejoiced in nature, breathed the air, and thanked God for another day.

Frank prided himself on being able to drive around in a nice car. He selfishly refused to let me share in choosing a more suitable car we both would enjoy driving. So he chose a Chevrolet Suburban on his own. Choosing to pick my battles with him, this was lowest on the totem pole. Maneuvering a large Suburban was tricky, and I was happier with my smaller car anyway. If this made Frank feel superior, so be it. I did not need material things to make me feel complete. One evening Frank was out on an errand, or so he called it. Calling him on OnStar, I was suspicious of his whereabouts. By the sound of his voice, I could tell he was up to no good. All of a sudden, a loud bang interrupted our conversation. Scared, I screamed, "What was that?" Frank nonchalantly responded, "Nothing." The next morning I went down to the garage to investigate. Knowing that Frank's word did not hold much clout, I wanted to view the car for myself. I had not imagined that loud noise and believed that he was covering up something. I noticed a slight dent on the front end. The Suburban was equipped with a black iron frame that protected the bumper, but a small collision was evident. Even though Frank adamantly denied any form of accident, I knew that he was lying. He never openly admitted the truth, but I was used to this and numb to his deception. I was thankful that no one was hurt. It appeared that the children were also quietly accepting their father's condition. Unfortunately, I think we all felt powerless. Unable to change him, we tried to go about our business and resorted to living daily without Frank. They still entertained friends and enjoyed teenage escapades. Their friends did not seem concerned that Frank was either asleep on the sofa or his recliner, and the girls didn't appear to offer any explanation. For now, they were content to escape to their bedrooms upstairs, away from the abnormality that existed on the couch downstairs. This was one time I appreciated innocence and naiveté.

Soon after, Frank decided to trade in the Suburban. He said that he wanted a smaller car, but I believed he was affected by the damage to the front end. Also, he had purchased this larger vehicle to accommodate the family on trips. Seeing how we had not taken any trips as a family, this idea was discounted. As a family, we visited the local car dealerships. Frank wanted us to make this decision together. Not surprisingly, the final decision was his. We settled on an Infiniti FX35. This was a beautiful car but much too expensive. I would have preferred a less costly model and could think of a thousand other things much more sensible to spend our money on. Frank did not value my opinion, and we drove off in a car that suited his needs.

Mindy, like most teens, was impressed with material possessions. Eager to show her girlfriend our new car, they dashed off down to the garage together. Within minutes, Mindy was quickly back upstairs, looking distressed. She disappointingly shared her story with me. Opening the skylight cover to the car to get a brighter view, Mindy was prey to two fallen plastic vodka bottles. Her friend knew of her father's drinking, yet Mindy was still so embarrassed. My daughter went from feeling proud to inferior in seconds. Knowing that it was not a reflection of her, she still associated herself with this disease because someone she loved and respected was letting her down, and she took it personally. We all did. Frank was not only hurting himself, he was damaging his entire family, and he was too sick to realize it.

You would think that I would be happy to hear that my husband might be on his way to an AA meeting, but this wasn't the case. Throughout the years, he did experience times of sobriety and until recently had been nine months sober. With evidence literally falling from the sky, I knew he was back to drinking. I can recall a time when I was still babysitting for my sister-in-law; Frank called and informed me that he was at an AA meeting. Doubtful, I asked to talk to one of his AA buddies. Frank did not attend meetings alone and always look forward to supporting members being there. He quickly replied, "Nobody wants to talk to you." Finding this hard to believe, I knew that Frank was lying. I had grown tired of repeating myself. Sounding like my African Grey parrot, I would demand, "You have to go to AA if you want to get better. You have to go to AA if you want to get better." I was beginning to think that he liked being ill because for him, it was much easier. In order to heal, Frank would have to endure pain and suffering, and perhaps he was too weak to submit.

If left untreated, alcoholism, like most diseases, will get progressively worse. Truly, I had no idea how to help Frank stop. I had tried threats, but they were unheeded. Faking calls to 9-1-1, I would roleplay these actions for Frank. My conversation with deaf ears would include my accounts of his verbal abuse and drinking. Believing me, Frank would take off running, and then jumping, over our six foot fence out back to escape. I knew this wasn't a joke but ironically, it felt like one. Here I was, a mature adult, playing games like a child. I thought I could trick him into quitting. Getting Frank arrested was an option I wanted to avoid because this would affect us as well. Also, I was afraid he would never forgive me if I went through with it again. There was a fine line separating Frank from a criminal. Arguably, his actions deserved punishment. I did not want to simply teach Frank a lesson by saying, "I told you I meant it. This time, I really did it." I needed to recognize that Frank had to do this for himself and not me. I was still waiting for the light bulb to go off in Frank's mind.

As I was finishing up my day at work substituting, I looked forward to the evening. We had planned to go out for dinner with my in-laws. Enjoying their company, I wished Frank could have inherited their sensibility. Perhaps by spending time together, Frank would someday recognize his parents' good morals and try to mimic them. When I came up the stairs and opened the door from the basement, I found Frank lying at the bottom of the stairway in our family room, leading to upstairs. His face was the color of cherries, and his body was motionless. I saw his chest rising and falling and knew he was still alive. Out cold, he was stone drunk. I grabbed my camera and clicked a few shots. I planned on sharing these disturbing photographs with Frank and hoped he would hate the way he had looked. Leaving him home alone, the kids and I still joined my in-laws for dinner. Picking us up, they too were angry and refused to come in to check on their son. We all assumed that he would be up and walking around when we returned and, frankly, had all had enough! Thinking back, I now realize this was the time I should have called 9–1-1. Frank was suffering from alcohol poisoning and could have died. His guardian angels were hovering over him that evening, and thankfully, he survived. Those telling photos were developed, and I showed them to Frank. However, they only served as a catalyst to make him angrier. I was not going about this the right way and knew it, yet I repeatedly made mistakes. My mind was reeling, and my emotions were high. I needed help and solutions, and I needed them now, before things turned fatal.

I found solace as I listened to my Christian music on my walks. The soothing melodies and inspirational verses put my mind at ease. Without faith, my ability to cope may have been hopeless. I was hopeful in one aspect, that being my children. I truly believed my choice to stay in marriage was beneficial to them. I toiled with the notion of leaving Frank and trying to support my children as a single mom. I wasn't afraid of hard work, but I was fearful that my absenteeism in the girls' lives would affect them educationally and emotionally. Reminiscing about my childhood, I reflected on my memories and remembered that my mother had often been absent in my life. She did not seem to have the time to talk to me about school or friends. I sometimes wonder if my choice to marry at such a young age was because I didn't seek my family's advice. I had grown up much too quickly, and I did not want my children to do the same. I wanted to guide and nurture them. I believed in order to accomplish this, spending time with them was essential. I wanted to oversee their homework, listen to their concerns, and cheer them from the stands when participating in sports. If forced to single-handedly raise them, my girls would need to forge their independence without me. Realistically, I knew my time was limited, and I had to contemplate this reality. I had to measure the importance of what would bring us the most happiness and believed that having each other outweighed being too consumed and not having time for my children. Crazily, this meant I needed Frank to be in our lives for financial support, even though it came with strings attached.

Desperately waiting to reach the light of a very dark tunnel, I still shone outwardly as a happy and content person. I knew that if I gave in to sadness and depression, my future would be bleak. I refused to bring my troubles to work, knowing that people did not want to hear about my problems when they probably had their own. If anyone needed sympathy it was Frank, not me. He had missed so much in his life, while I had experienced many pleasures. I had chosen not to hate him because deep down, I knew he needed my unconditional love. Believe me, I despised the man he had become, but I loved the person he once was. If I shared my story with co-workers, perhaps they would have disliked my husband, and I didn't want this. I wanted to introduce them to person I knew was hidden beneath a pool of alcohol. I needed to wait for him to be sober and still believed this day would come. Praying, I knew God would only give me what I could handle, and perhaps I had not reached this pinnacle. I would continue to listen to my music and find peace within the words sung and the feeling of hope those words provided.

12

Time was passing so quickly and along with this, the girls were getting older. My responsibilities outside the home were lessening, but I continued to keep a watchful eye on my children. Marissa, the youngest, was already in the seventh grade. I had just stopped teaching CCD but still valued all that I had learned along the way. I had a better awareness about my faith and was thankful for the opportunity to educate children who shared similar beliefs. I was better prepared to deal with my pain and sorrow, something I knew all too well, because my faith had made me stronger. Soon my faith would once again be tested and this time, it wasn't due to Frank.

My loyal and constant companion was showing signs of illness. I knew something was wrong with my Black Lab because one day when we were on our walk together, I had noticed his ears were dirtied with dried blood. Immediately, I had taken him to the vet. The doctor instructed me to start him on some steroids, hoping this would cure the problem. It was a Friday, and Maryanne was able to come home from college to be home with me. Frank was not offering any emotional support; therefore, I truly appreciated having my daughter nearby. Over the weekend, he had failed to show signs of improvement and appeared to be getting worse. My food-loving dog was not enticed by a hamburger. Obviously, something was very wrong. By Sunday evening, Maryanne had to return to campus. We prayed that our dog would recover but in my heart, I knew it was serious. On Monday, I returned to the vet with him, praying for a miracle. To my chagrin, I was not granted this wish. My beloved pet was suffering from a blood disease, and the doctor was not optimistic. The chance of recovery was slim. Most likely, he would get progressively worse. Amazingly, we were walking over four miles together less than a week ago. Now, my dog's precious life was ending. Not ready to say goodbye, I made the unpleasant choice of having to put him down right then. My heart was aching, but I knew I had to stop his suffering. This was something no one should have to do alone, yet I had to. With no one to lean on, I asked, "Frank, why aren't you here for me?" Selfishly, he had his bottle by his side, not his mourning wife. I will miss my best friend for as long as I live!

Already, the year 2005 was coming to an end. The older I was becoming, the more time sped by. As a teenager, I tended to rush the years away, always wanting to be older and more independent. Now, I wanted to slow things down. My topsy-turvy life had prevented me from doing all that I wanted to accomplish as an adult. I needed time, void from distraction, to organize my thoughts and dreams. A beach trip to Hawaii would provide a wonderful backdrop to ponder and contemplate my life. Frank had been planning a trip to Hawaii for us to celebrate out twenty-fifth wedding anniversary. I tried to put my feelings about Frank on the back burner. He was still drinking, I was sure of it. However, I was hoping this excursion in paradise together would bring us closer and make him more appreciative of me. Never did I expect to be boarding an airplane first class on my way to Honolulu. Our plans would include a night in Waikiki, followed by a cruise ship adventure to the other islands. It seemed too good to be true. We met a couple the first morning we were on the ship. They too were celebrating their twenty-fifth anniversary. Ironically, they shared the exact anniversary date as us. I believe it is a tribute to staying married for twenty-five years, especially in today's world. Take a look at Hollywood. We all laugh at the jokes put forth about Elizabeth Taylor and her many husbands. Longevity is not commonplace among the stars, but I do not believe that we should emulate that behavior. They say that life is not easy, and the same goes for marriage.

On our first adventure, we had planned on taking a helicopter ride over an active volcano in Kilo. To our disappointment, Mother Nature had other plans. It was raining buckets, and the pilot knew that the trip would be too dangerous. Our first excursion was cancelled, but I tried not to let it get me down. Looking forward to many more activities, I tried to focus on them instead. As we left the island of Kilo, the ship was steered as close to the volcano as safely permitted. We were close enough to see lava spewing down the mountain, which was really cool. Our next stop was Maui. We took a bus tour and arrived at the Haleakala Center. It was interesting, but I actually enjoyed the bus tour more. Later that evening, we went on a whale watch and sunset cruise. I marveled as these wondrous creatures swam in the ocean. I had never before seen a real humpback whale. As the sun set, I sighed at the beauty before me. To imagine waking up in such a beautiful atmosphere was a dream. Pinching myself, I knew it was a true. I didn't want this reality to end. Missing my girls, I wished that they too could have been here. The next day, we decided to spend a day of shopping in Lahaina. I wanted to bring back gifts that would symbolize Hawaii and share this experience with my family. We saw the most amazing Banyan tree. Planted in 1873, this tree was the largest in this state. These unique trees were very common among the islands in Hawaii and really piqued our interest. Captivated, we purchased a smaller version of this tree when we returned home. This house plant would serve as a reminder of my trip and the beauty of Hawaii. On our way back to the ship, we viewed several seals just resting along the shoreline. The closest I've come to a seal prior to this was at SeaWorld, and that was executed by staff. The natural occurrence and seeing them in their own habitat was amazing. I envied the people native to this island and imagined waking up every morning to such spectacular views. How lucky they are, and how fortunate I am for experiencing these unforgettable moments.

On the night of our anniversary, Frank decided to take me out for a special steak dinner. This was not part of our package deal but worth the added expense. Our meal was delicious, and I was happy to be sitting with my husband celebrating twenty-five years together. This was indeed a milestone, one not easily reached, but in my eyes, a testament to strength and fortitude. However, these pleasant thoughts were quickly interrupted by Frank's badgering. He was begging me to share a bottle of wine with him and using our anniversary as an excuse. We needed to celebrate and what better way to do it than making a toast. Willing to use soda or water as a substitute, I adamantly refused to drink with Frank. I knew this would send a message I didn't want to convey. I could tell Frank was having a difficult time abstaining from alcohol. The torment was written all over his face. Determined not to give in, I would rather have him angry than drunk. I won this battle, and Frank and I still had a pleasant evening. The tension remained, but I tried my best to change the subject and focus on other conversation.

While we slept, the ship traveled. It was so carefully planned and geared toward the travelers' experience. When we woke, we would be docked at a new island. We had planned our excursions prior to the trip, and for the most part, they were enjoyable. However, there was one activity I could have done without. Frank and I rode ATVs in Kona through gullies and over hills. Listed as a moderate (level two) for danger and difficulty, this ride, in my eyes, should have been rated a level three. Usually I pride myself on courage, but I could openly admit to being scared. Flipping it on its side, I

A DANGEROUS COMBINATION

was lucky I had not injured myself seriously. With a bruised leg and wounded ego, I couldn't wait for this to end. The sights were simply amazing but if I chose to see them again, I would do so on foot.

For the next two days, we enjoyed the island of Kauai. Perhaps my favorite, this island was truly splendid. On the first day, we hiked along a spectacular waterfall. After lunch, we were able to swim under the cascading water. This was one opportunity I could never enjoy back home. The landscape of Hawaii was so special and enjoying simple pleasures of nature was so easy there. We met so many other couples our age, enjoying the same experiences. I wondered if they felt like I did. If only we could bottle this and take it home. Snapping pictures like crazy, I would have to relive this through photographs. The second day on this beautiful island, we had chosen an off-road adventure. Thankfully our transportation, this time, had four wheels and was enclosed. I was not maneuvering over the rough terrain on a beast I could not control. Though bumpy, the ride was safe, and I felt secure as a passenger. This driver was skillful at handling the uneven turf, and I was happy to let him have the wheel. All good things must come to an end, true yet unfortunate. I wished my time there could have lasted forever. Too often, I have worried about what was happening next, rather than living for the moment. Today I am content to live for today and relish each and every minute. With so much to see and do, I would be crazy not to. On Saturday we left off the ship for the very last time and were on a bus to Pearl Harbor. Remembering what I had learned in school, I felt a stronger bond toward my country and pride for those who had lost their lives. After our visit, the bus drove on to the Sheraton Moana Surfrider, the oldest hotel on Waikiki Beach. We still had two more nights to stay and enjoy the beautiful beach which was walking distance to many sights. I felt relaxed among the atmosphere and was at ease. This sense of peace was something I had missed for so long and thoroughly felt I deserved. So much of my past was filled with uncertainties because of Frank's drinking. During this trip, he was in control and staying sober. He hinted about drinking, but I was resolved to keep alcohol at bay and out of reach. Thankfully, he relented and was seemingly on my side. We decided to wake up early our first morning at Waikiki Beach to enjoy the beautiful sunrise. Sounding like a good idea, Frank and I chose to spend our day relaxing on the beach. After some time, Frank was getting restless and decided to go back to the hotel room to check on his e-mails. Not surprised, I knew that Frank was not a beach lover, and I was happy to spend a couple of hours alone soaking in the sun's rays. Upon his return, Frank appeared different somehow. His demeanor, now changed, was that of a drunken man. I was certain he was intoxicated. If it walks like a duck and talks like a duck, then what else could it be? All too familiar, Frank the sneak was at it again. Pissed off, I charged back to the room right on his heels. I needed to confront him before he had time to sober up and hide any evidence. Sure enough, I found two empty pints of vodka under the bed. Screaming back and forth, we got into a heated argument, which included my accusations and Frank's denial. This is one picture I have too many duplicates of. I do not, however, have enough of that picturesque island. Therefore, I stormed out the door, alone, ready to see more of the scenery. Waiting patiently for the sun to set, I took in a little shopping. Buying myself a drink, I relaxed on a lounge chair, waiting for the opportunity to snap some photographs. Not disappointed, I gazed at the most beautiful sunset and captured it with my camera. Dreading heading back to the room, I knew I would have to inevitably see Frank and could not realistically avoid him forever. Making this decision with my head held high, I pushed into the room, met up with the enemy, and refused his invitation to have dinner together. I was not about to give in to Frank, not this time. Anyhow, I did not want his company, and for that matter, I wanted him out of my sight. Right then, his face was quite disturbing and made my stomach turn. I was content to close my eyes and go to sleep dreaming of Hawaii and the moments I enjoyed. This was our last night there, and he was not going to ruin it.

The next morning, we had to pack and get ready to leave. Even though Frank had attempted to ruin my last couple of days, he was not successful. I had grown numb to his disappointment and found solace in my own happiness. I was eager to get home to my kids and pets. I knew they needed me, and I was ready to return, even though I felt like I was leaving a piece of heaven behind. Frank was requesting cigarettes and an energy drink and decided to make a quick run to a nearby convenience store. Still angry from the previous night's events, I let him go alone. This was a big mistake! Who would think that a person ready to catch a plane and needing their senses would intentionally inhibit their abilities? Not I, but obviously Frank and I were not thinking alike. He came back from the store obviously inebriated. So much for trusting him!

The cab ride to the airport was excruciating. I wished I could have pushed my obnoxious husband out the car door. Oh, how I hated him when he drank. This was his rendition of Mr. Hyde. If only he would look in the mirror and acknowledge his ugly transformation. But the self-absorbed Frank would not allow this. Right then, I felt like I could not get home quick enough. Ironically, so much had changed, and a stupid bottle of vodka was to blame.

My kids and pets were ready to celebrate my return. My adoring Pekingese cried in my arms for five minutes. I was so thankful for my exhausted in-laws. For almost two weeks, they took care of my home and family. My children loved when they babysat, and I'm so glad they are a part of our lives. Unlike Frank, I wasn't ready to rush them out the door. He was pacing back and forth, practically counting the minutes for their visit to end. He was being so ungrateful. I did not want to spoil my in-laws' visit, nor worry them and chose to keep my feelings about Frank silent. I would share this with them in due time but for now remained quiet. I could literally count the seconds it took Frank to leave after his parents' departure. I was sure of his destination. Welcome home!

13

Frank's job provided several perks and one such opportunity allowed managers to use a corporate condo on the inner coastal waterway in Miami for one week every other year. This year, Frank planned a family trip during spring break since the girls would be out of school. Unfortunately, Maryanne would not be able to come along. Her college vacation was different than her sisters.' Mindy was excited when we agreed to let her bring a friend along. It had been quite some time since the family had vacationed together. Looking forward to enjoying their company, I was thrilled to have my daughters with us. They too had been through so much and deserved a little TLC away from home. I strove to bring normalcy to their lives even though their father was often drunk. For now, he appeared sober, and I was optimistic that he would stay that way. Hopefully, the children would provide the initiative Frank needed to make this trip a dry one. Our bags were packed, and we were all eager to escape the cool climate and bask in the warmth of Miami.

After settling in quickly, we decided to go out to an Italian restaurant our first night there. Even though Frank seemed edgy, he finally relaxed and enjoyed his meal. I instinctively knew that his mood was affected by his desire to have a drink, but I was trying to ignore my intuition. I was subconsciously crying, *please God, let him not succumb. Please open his eyes so that he sees what drinking has done to his life and ours. Let his love for us give him the strength to say no.* Thus far, my prayers were answered. The next morning, Frank and I took a three mile walk. We both loved to walk, and we talked about continuing this every morning while we were there. Our plans were simple, yet I couldn't be happier. I enjoyed a non-hectic day without time constraints and responsibilities.

Frank began acting aloof towards us as we were driving to Fort Lauderdale. Suspiciously, I questioned whether or not he was drinking. Usually this side of Frank surfaced once alcohol was part of his routine. It was like he was mad at me. I was a thorn in his side and standing in his way. Our day was far from perfect, but I did my best to avoid Frank's nasty remarks and unpleasant disposition. Our drive home turned ugly. Confused, Frank was uncertain of the route back to the condo and began taking out his frustrations on me. He began yelling, without regards to the fact that we had Mindy's guest in the car with us. I'm sure poor Mindy wanted to crawl under her seat. Remembering the embarrassment I felt as a teenager, I knew what this was like. We want nothing more than to impress our friends. Fighting parents can be impressionable, but not in a positive way. Thinking back, I should have forced Frank to let me drive because of his condition. Completely out of control, he could have easily caused an accident. I could not get back to the condo quick enough. To make matters worse, I later discovered that Frank had hidden a bottle in the glove compartment. From the air conditioning vents to the car, what next, Frank? Your secret was out but do you even care?

My dream had turned to a nightmare all because of alcohol. Spending our days on the beach, the girls and I enjoyed the daylight hours without Frank. He was too busy someplace else. As I lay on the warm sand, my insides would boil, and it wasn't from the heat.

He expected us to be all warm and fuzzy when he returned hours later from a day of drinking. I admit my reception was far from welcoming, and I didn't try to hide my feelings. Why should I? I was not putting on a false front for his sake. Perhaps I should have for the children, but my anger made this impossible. Frank had a way of breaking my spirit. I was actually better when he wasn't around. Ignorance is bliss, seeing how my reality was an intoxicated husband. I was inquisitive of Frank's desire to use the stairs rather than the elevator when leaving the condo. Tired of his denials, I acted like Sherlock Holmes searching for evidence. Behind one of the big pipes in the stairwell, I found a pack of cigarettes—Frank's brand—and an empty bottle of vodka hidden behind the pipe. Coincidence? I don't think so. It just so happened that we both made a pact to quit smoking way before this trip. He could not even stick to that promise. Besides hiding the fact that he was drinking, he was also sneaking cigarettes. I began to wonder whether Frank had any willpower. Like a raging lunatic, I confronted him. His good intentions always seemed to turned bad. Sadly, I unleashed my anger in front of the kids—something I was not proud of. I allowed him to bring me to this brink. Now, I appeared to be the instigator and the cause of turmoil. Hopefully, the girls were smart enough to recognize the truth and forgiving enough to accept my outbursts. Disappointingly, I wanted just to get home.

Leaving the next morning, I was reminded of our departure from Hawaii. Not much had changed. Once again, I called for assistance to take us to the airport. My husband was intoxicated and unable to safely drive his family. Luckily, this was already in our agenda for the trip. When we arrived at the terminal, I did my best to stay clear of him. The girls and I found our gate, and Frank found a bar. Innocently, I struck up a conversation with a friendly man about my age. He happened to be wearing a cowboy hat which, in most cases, would not attract attention. However, when Frank viewed us from a distance, I saw him glaring at us accusingly. Marissa was sitting right besides us. What did he think was going on? The man quietly remarked, "Is that your husband?" Embarrassed, I admitted that he was and also added that he was drunk. For some reason, I felt justified for speaking honestly. I was not about to make excuses for Frank's behavior. Not a moment to soon, our flight was called. Uncomfortable once Frank arrived, we were best to go our separate ways. Frank had turned our conversation into a liaison. Once seated, Frank repeatedly whispered, "Bubba, bubba" in my ears. Referring to the fact that this man had been wearing a cowboy hat, he was sarcastically ridiculing my acquaintance. Frank had a habit of putting others down. Perhaps this was his way of making himself look better. Actually, it did just the opposite. Frank was incessant with the name-calling, and I was becoming fed up. I walloped him over the head with a magazine that I was holding. He was shocked into silence. I hated turning to violence but could not think of another alternative. I couldn't get away from him like I should have, because of the tight quarters. Within minutes, Frank was sound asleep. Enjoying the rest of the flight in peace, I closed my eyes and thanked God that he was finally quiet. Frank woke up without any recollection of what had transpired between us. His attempt at being nice was not well received and did nothing to appease me. He had ruined our trip because of his selfishness, and nothing he could do or say would make it different. I did recall the time spent with the girls on the beach and smiled. Our memories were positive, regardless of Frank. Unfortunately, he would not remember much because his mind was skewed and his days were seemingly lost in an ocean of alcohol.

Frank was looking pretty bad these days. Therefore, his return to work did not appear very promising. Hiding behind his cell phone, he was fortunate that he did not have to come face-to-face with coworkers. It would be impossible to hide his intoxication. While I was at work, Frank and I would talk several times in the morning. By afternoon our conversations ceased, and he was no longer answering my calls. Finding it hard to focus, I would often confide in other teachers. Never judgmental, they offered their support and often shared their own stories with me. Somehow, this made me feel better. I knew I was not alone in my suffering and so many others had their own crosses to bear. For me, alcoholism was a demon my family had to face; for others, there were different hardships. I grew much stronger and wiser about life as I listened to others speak and offered my advice as well. In a sense, we all need each other. I knew I desperately needed time away from Frank and welcomed the company of others. Without this diversion, I probably would have gone crazy. I began to wonder if it was healthy in any relationship to be together 24/7. As the song goes, "Everybody needs a little time away from each other…"

There were times when Frank attempted not to drink. Doing this cold turkey and without medical supervision was not wise. Putting his dependent body into shock, he would suffer terribly from withdrawal. His body would ache, and most often, he would end up vomiting. This would last for a couple of days. I found it surprising to think that he would ever want to drink again. So deep into this disease, Frank was not aware of this futile attempt to stay sober and couldn't fathom that he would not be successful. Usually, within three days, he was back to the bottle, and this vicious cycle would begin again. Sure, he made promises to me to stop, but he couldn't stick to them. I began to finally realize that he didn't have a choice. He had harmed his body and mind so severely that he needed intervention from outside sources. I was not professionally suitable to offer the necessary aid Frank so desperately needed. Clearly, Frank's abuse was becoming a matter of life and death, and I was scared.

By this point in my life, I had started to feel alone. I began separating from friends and only really found solace in talking to my mother-in-law. We had this bond together and still shared a hope that Frank would recover. We knew that he had some sort of imbalance in his psyche that warped his thinking and altered his behavior. If we could only tap into his mind, perhaps we could figure out why he relied on alcohol. I still did not know what was causing him to drink. I chose not to burden my family with my continuing saga. My mother had been diagnosed with cancer at the age of sixty-two. She had thankfully recovered, but I knew she didn't need the added stress. Instead, I tried to sound convincing on the phone when we spoke. "Everything was fine; the kids were great," I would tell her. Sometimes my mother would question my responses. Perhaps she heard it in my voice. Still I reassured her everything was okay. I was starting to doubt my future with Frank. I needed to find strength and would pray all the time and always enjoyed the homily spoken every Sunday at Mass. I believed in the goodness of God and knew he had a plan for me. At this time, I did not know what it was, but I was sure he would guide me. Focusing on my good health, beautiful daughters, and the house we were so lucky to have, I realized things could be much worse.

Mindy, my middle daughter, was learning how to drive. She was growing up so fast. Luckily, I was able to spend so much time watching her grow. My husband was a failure in some aspects, but still he was a good provider. I was able to work when I wanted and was able to be there for the girls if and when they needed me. Many women do not have this luxury, and for this, I was blessed. I was also home to keep an eye on Frank. He was continuing to drink, and now he was driving intoxicated more than ever. I feared for his life as well as others.' Often, I would call the cops, hoping that they could catch him and take away his license. Ironically, I had a daughter getting ready to legally become a driver, and I questioned her maturity, and I had a husband who was much older but less responsible. Here I was, terribly worried for both of them. I knew I should not let my fear get in the way of my daughter, but I could try to stop Frank. Unfortunately, my calls to the cops were in vain. Frank was always one step ahead of them, and they were unable to find him. To some, I may have appeared crazy, but I knew better. Frank tried to convince me that I was to blame, and that he was a victim. I was smart enough to know the truth.

The summer of 2006 arrived. This year Maryanne would be turning twenty. Wanting to celebrate, she invited over a few of her friends. Everyone seemed to be in a festive mood, especially Frank. Unfortunately, he was amusing himself with alcohol and behaving like an idiot. Ordinarily, a birthday cake is a special moment for someone celebrating a birthday, but for Maryanne, this moment was far from special. Evidently Frank took it upon himself to take a piece of cake before we had a chance to sing and Maryanne could blow out the candles. I always thought the first slice was reserved for the birthday boy or girl. Maryanne was not given the opportunity to cut her own cake and make a wish. Obviously, these traditions were irrelevant to Frank. His idea of right and wrong were once again unclear because he was drunk. Bringing this to his attention later that evening, I attempted to explain this thoughtless act but was met with indifference. Frank was unaffected by my anger and did not believe that Maryanne was truly disappointed. In other words, it was not a big deal.

Like most summers, we were looking forward to our annual trip to Myrtle Beach. This year, Frank had plans to travel for business while we were away. I was relieved. He would hopefully be occupied with work, which meant he would need to stay sober. Perhaps I could finally relax on the beach with my family without being distracted wondering if he was at home drinking. Comfortable for a short time, I was soon forced back to reality. On Monday morning, my cell phone rang. Arriving home too soon from his trip, Frank had some news to share. While at the airport, he unknowingly had his suitcase and computer stolen. How could he be so careless, as if I didn't know. No one in their right mind would leave valuables unattended at a busy airport. I knew in my heart that Frank was not thinking straight, and I also knew why. His brother had to pick him up and drive him home because his keys were also stolen. Perhaps this was a blessing in disguise. He most likely was not in any condition to drive anyways. Even though I tried not to let it bother me, this did put a damper on the rest of my trip. I made every effort to put these negative thoughts to the back of my mind, but of course they were still there. However, we still had a good time. We were used to these dilemmas, and so was my family. Frank would have to deal with explaining this theft to his employer, since they provided him with the computer. I hoped they fell for his lame excuse even though I found it hard to believe. Keeping my feelings to myself, I would let him deal with the mess he created, as I surrounded myself with the people I loved and trusted most.

Being a mom, you always try to make things better. I knew that Frank's drinking was dire while we were away, but I didn't think it was best to get in the car, cut our trip short, and drive back home. That would not have been fair to me or the girls. I asked for their opinion because I wanted to know how they felt. They hated their father's disease, but they knew nothing they could do would change it. Returning home would not make a difference. Frank needed to do this for himself, not for us. We were his crutch, and he needed to walk on his own two legs. It was important to discuss any guilt we may have felt. When was the right time to say, "We are done enabling you to drink"? Were we turning our back on him, or was this necessary? How many more years would Frank miss seeing his daughters grow up? Time was passing so quickly, and Frank needed to act now, not later. Unable to turn back the clock, Frank would only have the future to look forward to, and right now, it did not look very promising for him.

My niece from Ohio was getting married in August, and of course, we would be attending the wedding. I would get the opportunity to see my family once again from up north. Sharing this special day with my niece was an opportunity I would not miss for anything. The kids would already be back in school; however, I was not going to let this stop us. Even Frank would be joining us this time. I had not intended for Frank to suffer such a serious injury right before the trip, but like most episodes in my life, I was used to the unexpected.

Just two weeks before we were scheduled to leave, Frank took a ride to the post office. He returned home extremely intoxicated and within minutes was sound asleep in his chair. Once he woke up, I was in his face, confronting him about drinking. I knew it would have been better to bite my tongue, but I found this virtually impossible. Talking to a person in this condition is like talking to yourself. Ignoring me, Frank staggered into the kitchen and grabbed his cigarettes off the top of the refrigerator. As he started to walk toward the back door, he lost his footage. He fell right into a ceramic plaque that was on my kitchen wall and with such great force that a piece broke off the plaque and cut his arm deeply. His forearm began bleeding profusely. Like he often did, Frank tried to lessen the damage caused by his recklessness, but I knew it was serious. I attempted but failed to stop the bleeding. I immediately called 9-1-1- to get help from the paramedics. Once they arrived and saw the seriousness of his injury, they suggested that he go by ambulance to the hospital. He refused their requests to take him. Instead, they did their best to bandage his arm and close his gaping wound. In the meantime, I had also called my in-laws, needing their support. Once his parents arrived and viewed Frank's arm unbandaged, they insisted that he go to the hospital. They would not take no for an answer. Finally, Frank was coaxed into going. He agreed to ride with his dad while I followed close behind. Once again, Frank was mad at me and refused my help. I was guilty and the cause of his injury. I knew in my heart the only thing I was guilty of was loving an alcoholic but dealing with his escapades wrongly. The doctors concurred and suggested surgery. Contemplating our trip, Frank decided to schedule surgery after we returned from Ohio. His injury was not life-threatening, and the doctors secured his arm with bandages. I was happy that Frank had reached this decision on his own. I didn't want to force him to come but was glad that he would be with us. He had watched my niece grow up when she lived in Georgia and should be there to share in her special day. Our trips to Myrtle Beach were yearly. This wedding would only come once. Frank had prepared a scenario to explain his injury and hopefully settle any skepticism. He had tripped over one of our dogs and fell. Most probably knew this was a lie, but Frank felt better thinking his secret was secure.

We enjoyed our niece's beautiful wedding, and I loved seeing my family. The long weekend sped by much too quickly. The only thing that seemed to linger was the nagging doubt I had about Frank. My thoughts were consumed with him drinking, and I was constantly watching his demeanor, hoping I could shed some light on this question. I had heard from others at Al-Anon that alcoholics often reach rock bottom before recovery begins. You would think that a chance of bleeding to death was enough to knock some sense into Frank. However, the surgery he faced was looked at by him like a mere setback. This was not a big deal. He still was neither ready, nor willing to face the fact that he had a drinking problem, and we were not through with the heartache of living with an alcoholic. It was as if everyone knew he had a problem—that is everyone but Frank. I could almost hear my family whispering behind his back. I wish instead they had the courage to tell it to his face. Perhaps this was part of the problem. They avoided the situation by denying that it existed. If only it was that simple.

14

Frank was out of control, and I needed to keep his insanity away from me. I chose three defense mechanisms to erase any negative feelings and prevent evil thoughts from entering my mind. Exercise, church, and music (104.7 The Fish) comforted me and acted as a type of natural tranquilizer that relaxed my nerves and soothed my conscience. The words sung by these Christian singers were inspirational (just a few of my favorites are Toby Mac, Kutless, Sanctus Real, and Matthew West) and made me aware that God has a plan for all of us, including me. While I may have wondered why he was testing me so much, I knew his intentions were pure, and somehow I was becoming a better person. I needed to stay trustworthy and maintain my faith. Without this, I would never have a chance of overcoming the hardships I was facing and would suffer even greater without God's helping hand.

Perhaps what disturbed me the most about Frank's drinking was his non-empathetic attitude about continuing to drive while intoxicated. I was scared to death that his irresponsibility would injure others. I was finding that my calls to the county police were becoming more and more frequent. On one particular day, Maryanne was home from college. She witnessed her father's erratic behavior and saw him flying down the driveway in his car, coming within inches of the mailbox. Maryanne was petrified that her dad would have an accident and took it upon herself to call the police. Frank had eluded the cops so often, I wondered if they would catch him this time. We told the officer that we believed Frank was on his way to the liquor store and relayed the make, model, and license plate number of his vehicle. Within five minutes, the police called back to tell me that they had caught him. Frank refused to take a breathalyzer and was arrested for reckless driving and given a DUI. My daughter Mindy's boyfriend was over and took me to retrieve Frank's car. Calling my in-laws, I was reassured by them that I had no other choice and had absolutely made the right decision. Frank was not only risking his life but selfishly placing innocent people in his dangerous path. Enough was enough. His brain had become so pickled by this dreadful disease. I prayed it was not beyond repair.

Frank's brother Bill went and bonded him out from jail. I was certain that my husband would be angry when he got home, and I knew he would rightfully blame me for calling. However, I did not care. I had grown beyond feeling guilty. He entered our home with his usual "I'm right" attitude. He informed me that he was prepared to fight the charges against him and had hired an expensive lawyer to defend him. It was like he was trying to get back at me. Because of my actions, our family would face this unnecessary expense. Holding my ground, I disregarded his ideas and kept telling myself, "He is a very sick man." If it helps, no dollar amount was too much to keep people safe from harm, and I would do it again if I had to. Unlike Frank, I did not need a lawyer to defend my actions.

The days passed by without much change. When I worked, I knew I would be greeted at home by my husband, either sleeping in his office chair or recliner. He would continue to hide vodka bottles, and I would keep on searching until I found them. He could hide all the bottles he wanted; however, he was not successful at disguising his intoxication. His unruly look and slurred speech were all the evidence I needed. He was so oblivious to people around him and was not raveled by my children's friends. He acted stupid in front of them as well. Thankfully, my children were noncommittal also. They did not allow his behavior to stop them from being kids and having fun. Basically we did our best to ignore him, careful not to rouse him. He was sleeping his life away, but we preferred him asleep rather than awake; this was actually less intimidating.

One morning, Frank asked me for his keys. Unable to come up with a believable excuse, he was probably intending on going to the liquor store. Because of this, I refused to hand them over. Frank was frustrated and bolted out the door on foot instead. The nearest liquor store from our home was at least four miles away. Certainly, he would not walk there. Quite some time had passed, and he had not returned. I made my way in the direction of the liquor store. Hoping not to pass Frank, I still wanted to believe that he was not that desperate. Unfortunately, he was. Pulling into a parking lot further down from the liquor store, I saw him walking toward our home. I did my best not to run him over, but that was how angry I was. He tried getting away from me with his liquor bottles stuffed up his sleeves. He looked ridiculous, and I wasn't much better. We were fighting like idiots on the side of the road. I was grabbing for the bottles, and Frank was determined to keep them. Finally, after quite a battle, I had successfully retrieved one of the bottles. Completely out of gas—me, not the car—I gave up and let Frank keep his bottle. I drove away leaving him behind. Deep down, I actually wished he wouldn't come home. That was how sad our life together had become. I hated myself for thinking like this, but I found it very hard to be in his company. When he arrived home, I went about my business and did my best to avoid him. I found that it was better to be civil. When I became out of control, it only escalated the problem because now my home had two irrational people. At least one of us needed to be sane for the sake of the children. If

I was too stressed, I would take it out on the kids, and that wasn't fair. Their lives were complicated enough.

Most nights, Frank would not make it up to bed and would instead sleep on the couch. Honestly, I didn't mind. I preferred the distance, especially because of his appearance. Sleep was not promoting a restful look for Frank. Instead he appeared haggard and worn out. Hours upon hours of sleep could not erase the aging effects of alcohol. How I longed to see the handsome man I had fallen in love with in high school. Frank's impending court date was weighing heavily on our minds. His future was in the hands of a judge. I decided to go with him to hearing. The verdict was handed down. Evidently they did not have enough evidence to charge him for a DUI, but they did get him for reckless driving. Somehow Frank felt victorious. He became cocky, promising to mail his lawyer a fine bottle of wine. Even his lawyer could see right through him. He looked at me sympathetically as if saying, "I'm sure I'll be seeing you again." Walking away, I was almost certain he was right. Frank insisted that we stop at the liquor store on the way home. He wanted to pick up the wine he had promised to his lawyer. Stupidly, I gave in to his request. I should have driven directly home, but I wanted to avoid a fight and believed my presence would hinder Frank from buying liquor for himself. I waited in the car. Surely, he didn't need a babysitter. Frank returned with the wine and a bottle of vodka. Although he attempted to hide his bottle, I was able to see it hidden under his jacket. I guess I needed to shadow him after all. Angrily driving home, I figured Frank was never going to learn. Ironically, we never even sent the lawyer the wine. When I brought it to the post office, they said they could not send it. By this time, Frank was already three sheets to the wind. I took the wine and figured I would save it for my parents when they came to visit. Looking at my drunken husband, I didn't know what else to do. Slowly, I was giving up hope, feeling more and more helpless. Even a court of law could not rightfully punish Frank. I began to wonder if he truly was invincible.

It was summer again, and the girls and I were once again going to Myrtle Beach. Frank planned on entertaining his fellow managers while we were gone. He promised not to drink in front of them. They were still oblivious to his problem, but I was concerned they would eventually uncover the truth. I was fearful he would lose his job if they found out how serious his drinking had become. His competency would certainly be questionable. He planned to enjoy the pool and cook on the grill for his guests. Wishfully hoping that this would occupy Frank, I left feeling less than confident. Arriving home back from our beach trip, I was greeted by a proud husband and clean house. He bragged that even the garbage was gone. His brother had taken it away because he wanted everything to be spic and span. Really, I thought otherwise. I imagined the trash contained evidence of drinking. Frank must have thought I was quite naïve. Regardless, I was happy to be home and see my pets. They were healthy and so were we, and that was most important.

Frank and his brother had to go out of town on business. Looking forward to enjoying the beautiful day, I invited a friend over to lay by the pool. Mindy was also home leisurely spending time with us. Wanting nothing more than to experience a good time with my daughter and friend, I was disturbed when I realized it was after two o' clock, and Frank was not home yet. Worried, I called my brother-in-law. He answered and replied that Frank should have already arrived. I shared my concerns with my friend, and she didn't look too surprised. For her, these episodes were second nature. All too often, I had ventured off looking for Frank. Many times, I found him sleeping in the car at our local grocery store. But still, I found it impossible to shake off this uneasy feeling and once again set out to find him. Steering toward the plaza, I saw his car in the parking lot. This time he was in front of Blockbuster. He was sound asleep, in the front seat, with the engine running. Peering inside, I saw a bottle on the floorboard. Using my own set of keys to unlock the car, I pushed open the driver's side door. After quite some persistence, I was finally able to waken Frank. Yelling at him, I demanded that he get in my car so that I could drive him home. The entire drive home, I accusingly screamed at him, and he remained quiet. It was like he didn't care. I remembered what some doctors had said, screaming does not solve anything. If this works with raising children, I suppose it would also work with adults. However, I found it difficult to reason with a drunk. Once home, I carried in his computer bag and luggage, leaving Frank to only worry about himself. Climbing the stairs from the basement, he slowly made his ascension. The fifth step proved pivotal. Unbalanced and unstable, Frank lost his footing and began falling backwards. The fall appeared in slow motion, yet I was unable to prevent it. I watched helplessly as my husband's head met the carpeted, cement floor. Screaming his name, I was uncertain of his condition. I anxiously looked to see if he was breathing and hoped the carpet had cushioned the blow. My girlfriend was still lying by the pool, so I rushed over to her side. I felt blessed that she worked at a hospital and was use to dealing with tragedies. I needed her calm and assurance. I was a basket case. I worried that he could be bleeding internally. I called 9–1–1 and within minutes, they arrived. They were able to make Frank responsive and began talking to him. He denied their request and refused to go to the hospital. Because of this, the paramedics did not have the authority to take him. They needed his consent, and he was too proud, or perhaps ashamed, to comply. Walking him over to the couch in the basement, they thought it was best for him to sleep it off. Obviously, they were not concerned that he had suffered a concussion. Following their suggestion, I accepted their expertise and medical advice. I was still shaking from the thought of losing Frank due to a freak accident. His drinking was making this more and more plausible. I know we all have a guardian angel, and I believe Frank's was working overtime. There is never a good time to lose someone you love and care for. And more importantly, someone you need and rely on. I felt like I was losing my husband, be it by death or divorce. I hated these scenarios and tried to push them away. I knew eventually I would reach a breaking point if Frank continued to drink; however, I just wasn't sure when it would happen or what it would take. I hoped never to find out.

Mindy's boyfriend Chris had a longhaired Chihuahua that he would bring over to our house. Soon, these visits were becoming more frequent. Chris lived alone and would have to leave the dog alone all day while he was at work. I know this bothered him, and therefore, he would leave the dog with us. I felt compelled to take the dog in. I asked Chris to let us adopt him. He quickly agreed, knowing this was best. This way, he could spend time with his dog when he was visiting Mindy and also eliminate the guilt of having a lonely pet. Now we were blessed with three dogs: two boys and a girl. They were small and manageable, but oh, so expensive. We constantly were doling out money for grooming and vet bills. Thankfully, the dogs were healthy. No major surgeries, for now.

Out of the blue my best friend from the past called me up to let me know she had cancer of the uterus. And would I please pray for her. She would be having surgery and hopefully the cancer is just contained in her uterus. I felt so bad, but I knew she be okay. Thank God the surgery went great and the cancer had not spread. This was our opportunity to become friends once again, and we both jumped on it. We played catch up on what we had done for the past three years since we hadn't been talking. Having her back in my life made me sure of God's perfect timing. Everything happens for a reason, and I know she needed a break from my chaos life. I missed talking to her every day, and I was sure glad she was back in my life.

Frank continued to work and travel on business. His true identity was a secret from his bosses, or so I thought. I found it surprising that they were not questioning his excessive drinking, nor were they suspicious of his demeanor. Perhaps he was that good at hiding it. While away at a fall convention, Frank's charade had finally come to an end. Apparently, his bosses had confronted Frank about their suspicions, and he adamantly denied it. He responded to their accusations by throwing his cell phone against a wall. Frank finally called me at four o'clock to share his version of the story. They were to blame; he was innocent, blah, blah, blah ... True to his nature, Frank was quick to blame others. They were onto him, and I was glad. Frank wasn't. And he was roaring mad. They were forcing him to attend rehab for two weeks on a daily basis. He would receive therapy all day and return home in the evenings. He signed on only to appease them and keep his job. Frank was still in denial and felt this was unnecessary, a waste of his time. I was thinking this was a step in the right direction. At this point, I was willing to accept any help. After two weeks, Frank completed the program, assured he was in control. Of course, I knew better than to believe this. Frank's dependence had grown too severe. A mere two weeks was not enough time to heal his body and mind.

Sadly, my predictions were correct. Frank was still drinking. His attempts to act sober were futile. Over the years, I had grown privy to distinguishing between a drunk and sober husband. My husband could fool himself, but he could not fool me. My parents had come for a visit. I was sure Frank could not hide his drinking from them. I hoped he would abstain from drinking to save himself any embarrassment. Leaving for work one morning, I was confident that my parents' presence would keep Frank on his best behavior. Unfortunately, I was wrong. Returning home from work, immediately I sensed something was amiss. My husband was obviously intoxicated, and my parents were not ignorant to his shenanigans. He tried to disguise the smell on his breath with a spray of Listerine. Instead, he smelled like a mixture of alcohol and mouthwash. It was like trying to hide a pervasive odor with air freshener. The underlying smell was still evident. At times the smell of mouthwash was so overwhelming that I thought Frank might be drinking it.

Without much thought, I began lashing out at Frank. Perhaps I should have considered my parents and their feelings, but I acted in the moment. Needless to say, a heated battle ensued between us. It became so intense, that my parents got involved. Frank's threats to my dad were so harsh that I decided to call 9-1-1. I was scared that his anger was beyond his control, and I feared for our safety. Soon thereafter, an officer arrived at our house. A creature of habit, Frank left and avoided the authorities. He was becoming quite the escape artist. If he was innocent then he did not have a reason to run. I explained my situation to the officer. Even though he was sympathetic to my plight, he could not do anything without the evidence, this being Frank. Waiting at the end of my road for some time, the police had no other choice but to leave. No one could say when Frank would return and the officer could only wait temporarily. After one hour, Frank finally returned home. Entering the house calmly, Frank apologized for yelling and swore he was not drinking. If only I could believe this. But deep inside, I knew he was a threat to himself and society. I did not want to bother the police, yet I felt responsible for protecting others. It wasn't like I was crying wolf. My worries were sincere. Unfortunately Frank was still able to stay one step ahead, but I knew eventually his luck would run out. If you play with fire, you are bound to get burned. I was determined to stay committed and put out the blaze. I felt I was the only one who could and prayed God would give me the strength to do so.

That Christmas, my parents came back to visit. I'm so happy that they did not stay away because of Frank. They were understanding of Frank's disease and sympathetic rather than judgmental. They too had witnessed the very generous and caring Frank in the past. While they were angry that he treated me disrespectfully, they were wise enough to realize that it was an imposter that was behaving this way. This stranger was controlled by alcohol. Optimistic, they tried to find the good in everyone. Perhaps this was where I had acquired this trait. During this visit, I began noticing a change in my mother. Yes my parents were getting older, but this was something different. My mom appeared somewhat confused and had a difficult time performing simple tasks. Later, I shared my concerns with my sisters. We were fearful that she may be suffering from the onset of Alzheimer's. We had lost our grandmother to the same disease years ago and were familiar to the warning signs. My mom, the retired nurse, frowned upon taking medication. She would even go as far to suffer with a headache rather than take an Advil. Because of her strong conviction, we knew she would be hell-bent on getting tested. Somehow, we would have to persuade her to see a doctor. I know she was scared of the results, but denying it would only further the prognosis. Like alcoholism, Alzheimer's can be an illusive disease because physically, you may appear healthy, but the effects are there mentally. On a positive note, Maryanne was finishing up her last year in college. Even with all the turmoil in my life, I had this to be grateful for. Survival would depend on what I focused on. To stay alive, I mean mentally, not physically, I needed to relish and celebrate the goodness in my life. I had a lot to be thankful for and would not take any of this for granted.

One Sunday, I let my dogs out into the backyard to enjoy the sun. We had just experienced a lot of rain and welcomed the drought. Finally, the dogs could run around in the fresh air. After returning from church that morning, I opened the back door to let them romp. I never expected this harmless act would cause such grief. I did not for one second believe that I had put my pets in harm's way. Apparently, the dogs had dug a hole under the fence that separated my neighbor's yard from ours. On the other side of the fence were two mixed breed labs that my neighbors two houses over had rescued. Together, my curious dogs were trying to see who was on the other side. The hole had become large enough so that my male Pekingese could wiggle his way under. A short time later, I was interrupted by my front door bell. I was greeted by my neighbor holding a blanket. Too my horror, my baby boy was wrapped in this shroud. Wandering into another yard, my dog had fallen victim to the jaws of much larger prey. Perhaps they thought my small dog was a toy. Looking at his lifeless body, I let out a shriek. Immediately, Frank and I grabbed him and rushed to the emergency vet, praying for a miracle. Out little dog was only four years old. I was imagining his chest rising and falling and pleading for him to breathe. Desperately trying to revive him, the doctors were not successful. My baby boy was dead, and I felt somewhat responsible. If only I had been watching, I could have prevented this tragedy. They had gotten out of my yard prior to this attack. Why hadn't I scrutinized the perimeter more carefully? In shock, I found it impossible to fathom. I would never see my dog again. Loving this dog like a child, I wept for days and days. Instinctively, I sensed that my female Pekingese was searching for her playmate. Running back and forth along the now repaired fence, she was barking and barking. It broke my heart. Hoping to mend her heart and ours, we bought another puppy. We hoped this new male Pekingese would somehow fill the void and lessen the loss we all felt. This new addition did relieve some of our sadness, but I knew he could not replace the dog we had lost. My female dog was still showing signs of mourning, but I hoped in time she would be as receptive as the Chihuahua. My neighbors could not be more apologetic. Just one week before this incident, their dogs had tried to attack and catch a squirrel. Questioning their aggression, they had to put them down to prevent this from ever happening again. Sadly, they too had to suffer a loss. Without animosity, I shared their sorrow and realized nobody intended for this accident to occur. I could not blame myself or others, but I would miss my dog so much. There are not any words to describe my pain. Oh how fragile life is.

15

I was finding it difficult to remain positive and was losing hope. I could not believe that Frank would still continue drinking even after all he had been through. From accidents, involving the authorities, and now even his employer becoming involved, what else could it possibly take for him to finally wake up? I had tried several approaches myself and was unable to change him. I knew that, for Frank, this transformation must come from within. He would need the saving grace of God. Praying, I asked for his intervention because not only Frank needed his help, I too was at my wit's end.

During February, I began working less and less. The stress was becoming too much for me to handle. While I wanted desperately to stay away from Frank, I found the separation caused too much anxiety. Thankfully, my job allowed me to pick and choose my days. For this, I was very fortunate. I had an appointment to get my hair done at eleven thirty on a Tuesday. Like most mornings, Frank informed me that he was running to the post office and picking up a breakfast biscuit. Knowing that there was some truth to this, I formulated my own scenario. He may have intended to complete the aforementioned errands, but I'm sure he should have included a stop at the liquor store. When he left, I tried to unwind and left for my walk. The morning was clear and cool, great conditions to think about and reflect on life. With Christian music playing through my headphones, I spoke to God like I often did. But this time it was different. As I looked up to the sky, I visualized the outline of a cross formed by the clouds. This image gave me such a sense of peace and relief. I felt that this was a sign from God who was there for me and was listening. I shared my sorrow and told him that I was at my end. I wanted him to take control of my life and guide me in the right direction. If he led me, I would follow behind. I needed his strength and wisdom because right now, I was incapable of making my own decisions. I knew I had choices but was unsure of which path to take. Frank was nearing rock bottom; yet with God's help, I knew things were going to be okay. I just needed to follow my heart. After returning from my walk, I got ready to leave for my appointment by eleven o'clock. Frank had not yet returned from his errands.

Leaving my neighborhood, I just started to pass by daughters' school. In the distance, I viewed a black vehicle swerving in its lane. The driver seemed to have lost control. Once the car veered closer, I was aware that the driver was my husband, not some stranger. His car hit a curb and was maneuvering on two wheels. Like in a dream, I felt like time was standing still. Hitting several more curbs, Frank's car finally came to a stop right next to a utility pole. This pole sat directly in front of my daughters' high school. Thankfully, the students were all inside. Pulling a U-turn to return to the scene, I parked my car and ran up to Frank. Pulling open the driver's side door, I was gazing at a very dazed and drunk man. All Frank could manage to say was, "What?" I couldn't say much either. I remember responding, "I can't do anything to help you, but hopefully God can." I returned to my own car and pulled into the parking lot of the high school. I was certain another vehicle would stop and call 9-1-1. I was too shaken, and I couldn't do it myself. I was scared to death, and I wasn't even sure what to say. Every ounce of energy I had was lost. All I could do was shake and wait patiently.

Snapping back to reality, I called the salon to cancel my appointment, and then I called Frank's brother. Still shaking, I began to actually feel a sense of relief. My brother-in-law patiently talked to me the entire time. No one was hurt, and soon the cops would deal with Frank. A small white car stopped, and the driver was dialing his cell phone. Within a few minutes, I expected to hear sirens. True to my predictions, a fire engine, ambulance, and two police cars dutifully arrived. The cops approached Frank's car, and I could see that they were attempting to persuade him to exit his vehicle. Not in any frame of mind to take orders, I speculated that Frank was obstinate. To gain access themselves, one of the cops took his billy club and busted through the back window. Watching, I observed Frank trying to restart his car. He wasn't going anywhere with a twisted front left wheel. Panicking, I didn't want them to hurt him. I only wanted them to help him. Finally able to get him out of the car, Frank was handcuffed. How surreal it was to watch someone I love being taken away and pushed into the back of a cop's car. This only happens in the movies. However, I knew this was inevitable. Eventually Frank's luck would run out. Watching the accident, I weighed the pros and cons. Seeing it firsthand, I would not have to listen to any of Frank's lies, but I would have to live with these horrible memories. I knew that I would often see these images play out in my mind for years to come. I still see my baby boy wrapped in that blanket. Now I would have to also remember seeing my husband in handcuffs being whisked away by the police. Shaking my head, and as if to erase these images, I only hoped and prayed that God would have more pleasant pictures in my mind to share with me in the future. I was definitely ready for a more pleasant sequel to begin.

While in jail, Frank made several attempts to call home, which failed. Apparently, there was a problem with me getting the credit card to go through to be able to accept his call. I called Frank's brother Bill that night to ask if he could pick him up from jail. The next morning, Frank arrived home. It only took minutes for him to start badgering me. I would not let him get the best of me and instead chose to ignore him. Becoming more furious, Frank stormed out of the house. He informed me that he was going to the store. I was sure I knew what this meant. Furious, I did not have any legal recourse. I could not stop my husband from leaving, yet I was almost certain he would come back intoxicated. I called my brother-in-law to vent and then called Frank's parents at the beach. I hated to bother them, but I didn't know who else I could turn to. They promised to be home as soon as possible to support me. The drive from Myrtle Beach would take close to seven hours. I knew it would feel like seven days. Not a moment too soon, they arrived. We pleaded with Frank to enter rehab but were greeted with a very vocal "No!" All Frank wanted was for his parents to leave. He couldn't stand the fact that we were all ganging up on him. Feeling their failure, his parents didn't know what else to do. They needed to return to the beach. They had fabricated a story about a funeral to support their quick departure. They didn't want to share the truth with their friends. Like I had mentioned earlier, my in-laws are private people. My parents were also at the beach during this time. I too chose not to burden them with Frank's issues. At this point, we all felt helpless. Why bother involving others and including them in our worry? They say that misery loves company, but this was not true. I was suffering enough, and so was Frank's family. It wasn't fair to let others feel this pain, especially when they too would be unable to stop it. My in-laws suggested that the girls and I leave our home and go to their house about thirty minutes away. They even said to take the pets. Contemplating their offer, I knew I should go but still hated the idea. Frank asked his dad to take him to the store. Against his better judgment, my father-in-law complied. We seemed to be throwing in the towel along with Frank. With only one working vehicle, I decided to quickly gather my belongings while Frank was gone. At least I would not have to worry about him driving while I was gone. My father-in-law returned home, but without Frank. He said he would walk home instead. Playing the victim, Frank was not getting any of our sympathy. Sadly, he was now on his own. Choosing the bottle over his family, Frank had driven me to this. Some may call it tough love while others may say I was running away, but I knew physically and emotionally, I had to leave. Frank was on the verge of falling off a very steep cliff, and I could not watch this happen. It was time for him to face his demons and leave us out of it. He would not be able to use me as an excuse any longer. The girls made plans with a couple of their friends to stay at their houses. I didn't want them missing school, and besides, they deserved to be around pleasant surroundings—something I could not offer right now. Calling work, I told them to clear my previous commitments. Also, I told them that I would not be available the rest of the school year. My grieving voice was hard to control. As I spoke, my cries told of my sorrow, and the secretary was sympathetic, yet non-prying. I wasn't ready to open up my heart to everyone and appreciated the privacy. I would miss working with the children, yet I knew I could not give them the patience and attention they deserved. Frank had gotten the best of me. Yes, I was down, but certainly not out. I was determined to get myself healthy and strong in case I lost Frank forever.

I received a call from the police while I was at my in-laws. My husband was found passed out behind our local grocery store. The officer asked if Frank and I had been fighting. Apparently, Frank used this as his excuse for sleeping outside. How pathetic. I'm certain the cops knew that there was more to Frank's story but did not ask for any more details. He had not committed a crime, but he was required to leave. I agreed that we had been fighting. They then asked where we lived and if it was okay to drive Frank home. Perhaps they wanted my approval because they wanted to ensure my safety. I responded, "Yes, bring him home. I am at my in-laws and out of harm's way." To think, my husband, a highly respected and successful businessman, had succumbed to sleeping outdoors and appearing homeless. On the contrary, he had a beautiful home and loving family to return to, if he so desired.

Maryanne drove over from college to see me. I could tell by the look on her face that she was as worried as me. Trying to console her, I told her that her dad's fate was in God's hands. These words also reassured me. Contemplating Frank's past DUI convictions, I knew it was not going to be easy. It was now time for him to face the consequences of his actions and abide by a court's decision. Whether it was lenient or harsh, he would have to live with the verdict. He was alive and able to work off his punishment. He was blessed to have that opportunity and should not take it for granted. Poor Maryanne had enough on her plate. She should have been focused on her studies rather than this. I reassured her that I was fine and encouraged her to go back to school. Her father had gotten himself into this mess, and only he could get himself out. The most we could do was pray, and that we did.

My kids called from their friends' houses that evening to keep me abreast of the weather. A severe storm had rolled in and was causing a lot of destruction in my neighborhood. I was not experiencing this at my in-laws but knew conditions were much worse at home. Now, I was beginning to get angry. The kids and I should be in our home, not Frank. I did not trust that he was taking any precautions to prevent any damage from occurring. Trees were coming down, and one could very well hit the house or pool. My sister-in-law came over to calm me. I shared my concerns. The weather was not the only circumstance creating knots in my stomach; I was also deeply worried about Frank. I knew his depression was severe, and he had made a couple of remarks about suicide. Whether this was a ploy, I wasn't sure, but I felt compelled to check up on him as well. Deciding to follow my heart, I drove home the next morning, praying the entire way. Not knowing what awaited, I was terribly scared of what I might find. My yard was completely covered in debris, but it did not look like any major damage had occurred. Now I had to find Frank. Anticipating the worst but hoping for the best, I opened the gate to the backyard. My eyes fell upon Frank. He was standing on the deck, surveying the mess. Immediately, my eyes welled up, and the sorrow and pity I felt for this man took over. To gather my composure, I took charge and began pulling some limbs from the pool. Trying not to focus on the mess, I turned my attention to Frank. Greeting him with niceties, I was prepared not to anger him. Deep inside, I hated him, or rather his actions, but chose not to relay this information. Rather, I spoke of my love for him and begged him to seek help. After at least an hour, he finally agreed. Knowing that it would take much longer then a weekend, Frank had to call his employer and tell them he was committing himself to rehab. Needless to say, they were not entirely happy but they did allow him a leave of absence. He had been working for them for over twenty years, and perhaps they felt his loyalty. They were giving him another chance but added that it was his last. Yes, it was Frank's last opportunity, but not to keep his job. More importantly, it was to save his life.

While Frank was receiving treatment, I was eagerly looking forward to some time alone at home. During this time, I could confidently say, "Frank was not drinking." The peace and solitude was wonderful; however, I still had my doubts. I would continue to stay optimistic and take one step at a time. One month might seem like a long time, but I knew it would speed by. I was allowed to see Frank once a week. I was met by a jittery husband on my first visit, but as the weeks went by, his appearance and demeanor improved. I did my best to speak positively and shared my opinions with Frank. He was so lucky to have an employer that was standing behind him. Obviously, they valued him as an employee. To think, how amazed they would be once he was sober. As the saying goes, you haven't

A DANGEROUS COMBINATION

seen anything yet. I hoped this was true for Frank's future as well as mine. I looked forward to a new husband coming home, one that I could trust and confide in.

Upon arriving home, Frank continued treatment by attending AA. The dreams of the past had finally come true. For so long, I had wished Frank would take the initiative and submit to receiving help from others who also shared his disease. It would be possible for him to relate to others who suffered from the same addiction, share in their struggles, and celebrate victories. One such person Frank was fortunate to meet was a man named Dan. Quickly, Dan became a member of our family. He had been married a few times before but was now divorced. Together, he and Frank would go to AA—something I was happy about. While it did not guarantee Frank would continue to go, Dan's company made it much more plausible. Finally, Frank had a friend that supported his efforts to stay away from the bottle. He was no longer fighting this battle alone but instead had a friend who was also combating the enemy, alcoholism.

While Frank was away on business, I decided to take advantage of the beautiful day and work outside in the yard. For some time, Frank had been complaining about the dogs going through the bushes out back. I wanted to purchase some cheap fencing to protect the bushes and keep the dogs at bay. Home Depot was close to our house, and I planned on making a quick trip. I left the dogs outside for this short time because I did not feel it was necessary to lock them in their kennels. After making my purchase, I made my way home. Heading down the hill toward my house, I observed four cars stopped around something in the middle of the road. I noticed that their eyes were fixed on a white puffy figure lying still. The first thought that jumped into my mind was that my baby girl had snuck out beneath my fence. Please God, don't let this be true. I knew she still desperately missed her brother and was always looking for him. Her small stature made it easy for a driver to overlook.

My worst fear proved true. It was my dog lying there. The driver of the vehicle had left the scene, but my neighbors were there guarding her. Her tiny fifteen pound frame seemed lifeless, but I saw her big brown eyes looking at me. Thank God, my girl was alive. Gently picking her up and cradling her in my arms, I noticed that she was not bleeding. However, I knew her injuries were severe. My caring neighbors offered their support, but I assured them I was fine. I had to check on the other two dogs before leaving. Finding them safely confined behind the fence, I quickly put them in their kennels and immediately drove to the vet. I cried and prayed hoping we would not lose her. She was unable to stand on her hind legs, and I questioned the possibility of internal injuries. The doctor took over, and x-rays were taken. They said it would be some time before they reached any conclusions and assured me that they would call me as soon as they read the images. Waiting for the doctor's call was sheer torture. Fortunately, Frank was there for comfort and support. Still out of town, he stayed on the phone with me and said he would support any decision to save her, no matter the cost. That was what I wanted to hear. My husband was rational and supportive in this time of crisis. His sobriety was a gift I desperately needed, because I couldn't handle any more stress, especially now. Finally, the doctor called and said the x-rays showed that her pelvic bone had split and one leg was broken. Her next words were music to my ears. There was not any evidence of internal injuries. With surgery, her pelvic bone and her leg could be fixed, and after six weeks of rest, her recovery looked promising. She was scheduled for surgery the next morning, but not at the same clinic. We were allowed to take her home for the night. She wasn't able to walk, but all that mattered was she was alive. I immediately fixed the loose board that had allowed her escape. The discovery came a little late and the damage had already been done, but placing blame was not going to do any of us any good. Instead, we learned a valuable lesson and could only avoid the same mistakes in the future. With a successful surgery, my bandaged dog came home. The doctor did order strict follow-up care. She was not to run or play for six weeks. I knew that being kenneled would seem like a punishment, but it was important for the healing process. With our impending trip to Myrtle Beach, I had to make a choice, and I did. She would be coming along with the girls and me. Still in solitary confinement, my little girl could not play along with her brothers. I didn't trust that Frank was up to the task of her constant supervision and felt better to keep her with us. The girls were all too happy to have her along. We all loved her and were so thankful we were spared from losing another dog. This thought sickened me, and I would do everything in my power to prevent it from happening again.

Planning for our trip, I was still somewhat worried. However, with a DUI hanging over his head and the knowledge that his employer knew about his drinking, Frank certainly would not take any chances. That would be simply stupid. Dan promised to keep Frank company while we were gone. I was hopeful that his presence would lessen Frank's temptation to drink. He should be too busy entertaining his friend, as well as keeping up with work. I was sure they were measuring his performance, as well they should. He had responsibilities to fulfill, and they expected him to give 100 percent. The girls and I were anticipating a relaxing visit to the beach, considering these conditions. I would not need to worry about their father, and in turn, they could enjoy a stress-free mother. Within forty-eight hours upon arriving, everything changed. Frank was not receiving nor returning my phone calls. Warning bells were ringing. When we talked, the few times we did, arguments ensued. I knew that calling Dan would be fruitless. Frank would not listen to anyone when he was drunk, not even his closest confidante. Instead, I called Mindy's boyfriend. I asked that he go to my house to retrieve the two dogs. I did not trust that Frank was caring for them, and after the last tragedy, I wasn't about to let his negligence threaten their well-being. The last two days of our vacation felt like an eternity. I was anxious to get home and check on Frank's condition, and for that matter, my home. I was comforted in knowing my dogs were safe. To think, Frank had disregarded all threats and selfishly continued to drink. His job and freedom seemed inferior to what he held highest. What could it possibly take for him to stop? I had thought his future, as well as his family, and the fact that we may not have one would be enough. I guess I was wrong.

Pulling into the driveway, I realized that our new car was missing and assumed Frank was also. As we were unloading our belongings, I saw Frank driving by our cul-de-sac. Frank quickly pulled a U-turn as if he was leaving the neighborhood. He hadn't seen the girls or me in a week and was doing his best to get away. This was too much to bear. Once again, I was determined to get him off the road. Trying to chase him down with my car, I saw him turning back into our neighborhood. However, he was not turning down our street. I stayed and blocked the street, making it impossible for him to leave. First, he would have to get by me, and I was not budging. Coming to a dead end, Frank was forced to turn around and stop. Screaming at the top of my lungs, I demanded that he get out of his car. My voice must have been quite loud. My neighbor, the one whose Christmas party we had attended, came out of his house to check out the commotion. Once a good friend, he knew Frank had a drinking problem, but he wasn't aware of the severity. He was kind enough to try to help. After talking with Frank, he persuaded him to exit the car. Together, the three of us drove to our house. Patiently, our neighbor tried talking to Frank. I'm not sure if it did any good, but I did appreciate his effort. Later on, Frank admitted that the entire week was a mystery. He had no recollection of what had transpired or where the days and nights had gone. He had had a total blackout. Now, I was scared more than ever. Was there any hope for Frank?

16

I was shocked and disappointed to see Frank once again in this condition. With the DUI weighing heavily on his future, I could not believe that he would jeopardize his chances by continuing to drink. I was sick of him ruining my trips to Myrtle Beach. Luckily, the children were unfazed. They were numb to his behavior and had learned to block out their father's inhibitions and just enjoyed fun times with their cousins. I wish I could say the same, but in truth, my spirit was affected. Sure, I did my best to ignore the uneasiness, but it was difficult. Fortunately, my family was understanding and sympathetic. I would have been lost without their support and was thankful that they remained nonjudgmental.

The look on Frank's face told a very sad story. He felt awful about his inability to stay sober. He truly enjoyed his sobriety, that I knew, yet he continued to fall off the wagon. Looking for answers, Frank went back to see his doctor. Thus far, his doctor had prescribed the drug Campral, which was intended to dull the receptors in the brain that made Frank crave alcohol. Apparently, this was not working for him, and obviously something else was needed.

This time, the doctor was able to shed some light. His diagnosis was quite surprising and unexpected. He concluded that Frank was bipolar. Ignorant to such an illness, neither Frank nor I were educated about this disorder. My husband was forty-seven years old and had just found out he suffered from an affliction most of his life. He was categorized as bipolar I, meaning he experienced more manic episodes. Evidently you were either manic or depressed. Knowing Frank's personality, I would strongly concur with the doctor. The doctor strongly recommended that we read about this illness to better understand Frank's moods and how to treat this disease. The first step was to get Frank on some medication. The doctor prescribed the drug called Geodon. Almost at once, Frank began showing signs of calmness. In the past, he could have worn out the floor with his pacing; now he appeared more relaxed. Relieved, we wanted to share the news with his parents. Knowing there was something wrong with Frank, we now had a name to refer to. They say that ignorance is bliss. In this case, I would disagree. We all felt more assured now that he would be taking the proper medication to stabilize the chemicals in his brain. To learn more about his disease, Frank took the doctor's advice and purchased a book called "Bipolar for Dummies." Upon reading, we discovered that Frank's personality matched much of the characteristics described for those diagnosed manic. One particular trait stuck out, "No matter what bad things I do, I'm still a great person." Some others said, "I'm always right. I'm amazing. Everybody loves me. I'm the fastest at everything I do, and I can do anything and everything." It was ironic that these traits all suited Frank to a tee. If only we had discovered this sooner, perhaps he would not have chosen to self-medicate. With our newfound knowledge, we were better prepared to deal with his disorder, relying on the doctors to prescribe the proper medication and assuming the task of learning more.

The doctors chose to also prescribe the drug Lamictal. They were upfront and spoke openly about the uncertainty of getting it right immediately. It would take some time before the proper mix of drugs and dosages were properly suited for Frank. Each case was different, and every patient responded differently. After all we had been through; we were ready and willing to wait it out placing our faith in the doctors hopeful that eventually the perfect combination was found.

Ready for an excursion and some fun, Frank, Dan, and I planned a trip to Florida. Fascinated with the psychic world, I heard about a spiritual camp that was located there. For years, I watched Sylvia Brown on the Montel Williams show, even going as far as taping it. I was amazed at her abilities to describe and speak about strangers' lives. She gave so many hope and for some closure. Being a Catholic, I was aware that worshipers of this faith were encouraged to stay away from psychics. However, I believe God has a purpose for all of us, and psychics have the gift of talking to spirits. I did not view them as evil and found their intentions were good. Happy with my life, I was just looking for a little adventure and perhaps some hope for the future. Maryanne had graduated college and would be home to stay with her sisters. With everything in place, we left. Driving together was a blast. Frank and Dan had me in stitches. Frank was quick with his wit and so was Dan. The two of them made jokes the entire ride, making it lively. It felt so good to laugh!

Frank professed that he did not believe in the psychic world and was only coming along for the ride. Happy to have his company, I was fine with this. Dan and I were more accepting of this spiritual phenomenon and ready for our reading. Perhaps Frank would change his mind. I realized that this trip meant more to me than just meeting psychics. During this time, I rediscovered the love I had for my husband. I mentally visited my wedding vows and replayed the words in my mind. For better or worse, sicker or poorer, till death do us part! I had chosen to stay with Frank and together, we had found that he was indeed sick. If I had divorced him, we may not have ever discovered his disorder, and his future may have been fatal. I did not think every partnership was the same, nor should every couple stay married. Each circumstance is different. However, after talking to many divorced people, I found that many chose to separate because they thought their lives would be better. For many this was unfounded. The grass may have appeared greener for some, but after divorcing, they discovered that this was not the case. For many, the work only got harder and caring for their family independently was a struggle, not to mention lonely. Like most decisions in life, it is better to weigh the pros and cons, rather than acting in haste. There will be less chance of regret.

Beforehand, we had done some research on the computer to check out the available psychics. Frank chose one that sounded great to both Dan and me. Still unconvinced, Frank said he would see her first, then Dan and I would follow. I was glad Frank was willing to take part. Having been a witness to their readings, I was hoping Frank would also discover the gift that some psychics have. I was wishful that they could foretell his future and share scenarios that were positive and that painted a bright future for him, even though he was facing a tough road ahead.

While Dan was seeing the psychic, I decided to kill some time waiting for my appointment. I sat while a psychic read my tarot cards. I listened and respected his interpretations, but I was anxious to see my scheduled psychic. When this reading was done, I drove to where Frank was. The look of shock on his face made me curious. Something was told to him that caused this reaction. With my fingers crossed, I listened to the results of his reading. When Frank entered the room, the psychic asked for one item to hold. He gave her the cross that he always wore. Holding it tightly in her hand, the psychic told Frank something astonishing. She said, "You will be seeing a judge, but it won't be as bad as you think." He had not mentioned anything to her about his upcoming trial. How could she possibly know this? She also spoke about other revelations that made my husband think twice about his skepticism. He was actually so moved that he left before his reading was over. Frank was not quite ready for this; however, I was and anxious for my turn. With the good news Frank was given, I also hoped to hear encouraging words.

Like Frank, I was asked to give her an item I held dear. Handing over my beloved grandmother's ring, I knew this was closest to my heart. Closing her eyes, the psychic responded, "You are a teacher." I replied, "I am a substitute teacher." She then added that she sees me working with kids with special needs. Hitting it right on the nose, she was correct in this assumption. Most of my days subbing were in a class reserved for these children. Many teachers do not want to work in this classroom; however, I found it extremely rewarding. Finding this admirable, the psychic told me that I should also consider working with high school students. She said the older children really enjoyed listening to my advice, even though my own girls would strongly object. They said I act like "Miss Know It All." I was happy some kids valued my advice. I had learned life the hard way; I hoped my experience would educate them to make theirs a little easier. She then offered, "You have a bird. He is a happy bird." Right again! I then said that I would like to know something about my daughter Maryanne. She said, "Do not worry. Soon she will go on a workout regimen and lose a lot of weight." With her recent graduation, Maryanne would be making significant chances in her life; I was happy this meant a healthier lifestyle. I wanted her to share some information about family members that had passed on. She said there was an attractive older woman who watched over me. Telling her this could be one of several people, she wasn't able to give that person a positive identity. I wanted to hear more about my aunt who had died from cancer. She wasn't able to share much about her. Still happy for what she did share, I left feeling content. The premonition regarding Frank was enough to make my heart skip a beat. Perhaps this day was meant for him, and for me, that was perfectly okay.

Returning home, my feelings of uneasiness reappeared. They say that old habits die hard. Boy, was that true. Even though Frank was habitually taking his medication, I feared he would once again drink. Also, his upcoming court date was bearing down on us. I tried to hear the words that the psychic spoke: "It's not going to be as bad as you think." Growing weary of constantly worrying about Frank, I recounted my faith and put my trust in God. No matter what the outcome was, I knew he would be there for me and my family. I had to live for today, enjoy the moment, and remember that every day is a gift.

I had to travel up to Rhode Island to celebrate my parent's fiftieth wedding anniversary and my mother's seventieth birthday. I would be traveling alone, leaving Frank and the girls at home. I was nervous that Frank would suffer a relapse while I was gone, but I wasn't about to let this stop me. My mother's disease was progressing, and together, my parents were sharing a milestone. Because of this, I needed to be there. I did not know how many more years I would have with them. I wanted to remember them as healthy and coherent. I wanted to rejoice in life while everyone was still around to be a part of the memories; often we wait too long. After I returned home from a relaxing trip, it was wonderful to see Frank was well and sober. Life remained calm!

Another year of holidays was approaching. With the courts so busy, we had not yet been assigned a date for Frank's hearing. I continued to focus on the positive aspects of our lives. Frank still had his job, and we were all healthy. I could not ask God for anything else.

Already, the year 2009 was upon us. Looking back over the years, it seemed like I just had my girls and I was busy taking care of babies. Now, my second born was graduating high school. Time was flying by. Frank was suffering side effects from the drug Lamictal. His face was covered in a red rash, and the skin was peeling. The doctors realized that his medication would need to be changed.

Care must be taken when any of these drugs are prescribed. We were quickly learning about the dangerous side effects, even fatal, that could result if proper dosages were not taken. For example, the doctors then prescribed Frank Lithium. Skeptical that Frank was drinking, I went as far as making him blow into a breathalyzer we had purchased off the internet. The results proved that my speculation was untrue. Something else was causing him to appear drunk. Revisiting the doctor, we discovered the dosage of Lithium was much too high for Frank's body to handle. The doctor smartly lessened the amount prescribed by one-third. I knew now that what the doctors had previously said was true. It would take time before the correct mix of medication was successful for treating Frank. With Frank's impending trial, I was praying feverishly that the doctors soon got it right. Frank needed to present himself as stable and competent before the judge. His future could depend on it.

This year, the holidays were even more special. With Frank's sobriety, it was a thrill to have my husband around to share in the joy I felt every year. Seeing the look on my children's faces made me forget that my husband was an alcoholic and most of the time drunk. This Christmas, my elation was even greater. At long last, my husband was a part of our day in every way, sober and sound. Our home was much more serene. The only chaos that occurred was fun-loving and welcomed.

Another obstacle that had to be conquered was my addiction to tobacco. After trying several times to quit on my own, I decided this time I would seek assistance. I was all too aware of the dangers of smoking, yet I was still unable to quit. With Ash Wednesday approaching, I wanted to give up cigarettes for lent. My ob-gyn prescribed the medication Chantix to help me overcome the desire to smoke. I would need to take this medicine for three months. The pills, coupled with prayer, have helped me stay smoke-free thus far. Remembering my girls, I never want to jeopardize my life and risk the chance of never seeing them get married or experiencing the love of grandchildren.

My daughter Marissa's best friend's mother was planning a wedding in Florida. Her future husband was a friend of five years. They planned on exchanging their vows on the sands of the beautiful Ormond Beach. This was only about ten minutes from Daytona Beach. At first, we hadn't planned on attending. I was so happy for my friend, but the expense of another trip to Florida so soon was challenging. After finding out that Marissa would not be able to go because she needed a ride home, Frank and I changed our minds. Instead, we would drive down ourselves and later bring her back. I was happy to be there to celebrate with my friend. Frank was not much of an acquaintance of her, yet he said he would come anyway. He asked Dan to come along. While I was at the wedding, he and Dan decided to do some deep-sea fishing. Because Dan was coming along, we made appointments to see the same psychics. The spiritual camp was only thirty minutes away from our hotel. Excited, I looked forward to another trip, a beautiful wedding, and another reading.

We arrived to Florida on Friday with the wedding planned for the following day. As intended, Frank and Dan enjoyed a day of fishing while I was entertained at my girlfriend's wedding. The following morning was Palm Sunday, so I was excited to find a Catholic church directly across the street from our hotel. I had anticipated missing Mass and felt somewhat disappointed. It was interesting to attend other churches and experience different homilies. This trip was such a blessing, and I felt a need to extend my gratitude to God. We would also be seeing the psychic that day. Nervous yet eager, I intended on questioning her about Frank's upcoming hearing. I knew I needed to have faith, and I also played back the last psychics words, but you can never have too much reassurance. Once Frank was finished, I had my opportunity. I chose my wedding ring for her to grasp during the reading. Her first words were, "You are very organized and plan your days in advance." Yes, this was true. I then said that I was worried about my husband. Her response was, "Do not worry. His job will not discover anything about his mishap, and soon things would be much better for Frank." In addition she told me, "Eventually, his employer will gain back their trust in him and appreciate his performance." This would be wonderful. Knowing how much he loved his job, I was relieved that his future looked promising. He would be devastated if they let him go, especially after twenty-five years. I so much wanted to trust her, but I must admit, there still was some doubt. She added that she was aware that Frank took me for granted over the years, but he really did love me. Over time, his love would only get stronger, and he would be more committed to me and our marriage. This was good for my ego. The hurt I felt when Frank belittled me in the past still remained in the back of my mind. I knew that was the alcohol and not him speaking but it was still demoralizing. I looked forward to a new relationship based on equality and respect. Next, she said that she saw me writing. I thought that was crazy. I had never really spent much time reading, and now she was telling me I should be writing. Not quite sure of this, I didn't really ponder her words at that time because to me writing was foreign. She explained that I was listening to music and dancing around the house. Yes, this was something I did while cleaning. To end this reading, she shared her notion that the spirits said I was living my life right. I hoped so. While not perfect, I do try to live morally and make good choices. Thinking back to watching Sylvia Brown, I only dreamed of sitting before a psychic and listening to her words. I was blessed to have this opportunity twice. I felt much better when we departed, thankful for the encouragement and more prepared to face the uncertainties and struggles that may lie ahead.

17

Soon after we returned from Florida, the letter finally arrived by mail. Frank's court date was set for the middle of May. The accident had occurred fifteen months prior, and we were ready to rid ourselves of this memory. Without knowing Frank's punishment, this was difficult. However, we were ready to know our future. We dreaded the consequences yet felt we needed to put a period at the end of this very long saga.

I had already committed to working for two weeks in May for one of the special education teachers. Therefore, I would be busy during his hearing and unable to physically support him. That day dragged on as I was nervously anticipated Frank's call. I agreed that his punishment should be strict, yet I was scared for our family and what this could do to us financially. The prosecutors were asking for three years with one and a half years to serve. I know that Frank's undiagnosed illness made him react irrationally, yet we had to live with the decision. Frank was the primary supporter for our family, and if he was in jail for a long length of time, his employer would most likely fire him. While I tried not to contemplate this, it was very plausible, and therefore, the waiting was excruciating.

I could only imagine what this would mean to my daughters and their emotional and educational futures. At two o'clock, Frank called with the verdict. He was to be taken directly to jail, where he needed to complete a ninety day prison sentence with forty-five days to serve. He asked the courts if they would consider permitting him to divide his time between three fifteen day stays. Luckily, they agreed but still we were not sure his employer would allow him any additional time off because of his last request for a month in rehab. They were ignorant to his DUI, and we preferred that they remain this way. Because Frank was expecting some jail time, he did not yet take a two week vacation he still had available. He called work to say that he would be taking this vacation but did not offer anything further. We needed to take one step at a time. The thought of him in jail made my heart ache and stomach turn, but I knew it could have been worse. I still had my husband. He was being treated, and for now, his job was secure. I chose to share this news with only a few of my family members and closest friends. This was my business, and I wasn't ready to openly share my life. I had to deal with the I should have or could have, etc. I did what I thought was best for me and my family, and that was all that truly mattered.

Leaving work, I drove to the prison to take Frank his medication. That was when reality hit me hard in the face. This was perhaps the saddest day of my life. So many years had passed since I left my home state and family behind. But today, I felt the loneliest. Sitting at home by myself outside, I thought about Frank, his imprisonment, and what explanation he would give to his employer for the remaining thirty days. All of a sudden, a flock of cardinals arrived. There were at least eight birds perched in my backyard. Smiling, I greeted them and acknowledged their company. My guardian angel was there saying, "Everything will be all right." This was Frank's favorite bird, and they had come to tell me he was okay and I did not have anything to fear. I have never again seen so many cardinals come at once and believe this was a sign sent from above to give me peace and hope.

Ironically, I began to enjoy the tranquility over the next two weeks. For the first time, I could rest knowing Frank was not drinking. Before, I never was 100 percent guaranteed.

Frank had finished his first two weeks in jail but was required to serve thirty days more. He pondered on what he should tell his employer. I knew this weighed on his mind, but I was suspicious of his behavior. Sleeping at different times throughout the day, I knew his anxiety was not enough to cause this magnitude of sleepiness. Could he possibly be drinking? Requesting a breathalyzer, I demanded that Frank show proof of his sobriety. Continuously, it registered zero. Confused, I was determined to get to the bottom of this. Calling Frank's doctor behind his back, I shared my concerns. I wasn't able to tell Frank initially about the call because I knew what his response would be: "Do not get involved. I'll be all right." The doctor made us an appointment for the following day. Once the appointment was made, Frank had no other choice but to go. Unknown to me, Frank had also been prescribed an anti-anxiety pill called Xanax. Highly addictive, this drug can act negatively if the dosage was exceeded. Frank was obviously taking too much. Weaning him off Xanax, the doctor chose an alternative drug. The difference in Frank's demeanor was night and day. He no longer portrayed behavior similar to being drunk. Ironically, this was the effect Xanax had on him. Thankfully, this problem was alleviated. While we were in the doctor's company, I shared our story with him. He had the intuition to offer us a plausible excuse for Frank's thirty day prison sentence. He recommended that we tell his employer that Frank was asked to partake in a thirty day rehab for people suffering from bipolar. Sounding like a good idea, Frank did just that. They believed his alibi and gave him the necessary time off. While lying was not something to be proud of, we knew that his employer would not be so compliant if we told them the truth. In a sense, Frank was attending rehab. Prison for him was a foul dose of medicine that he never wanted to take again. I firmly believed God had put him there to show him that if he chose to drink again, this would be the consequence. Learning the hard way isn't fun, but for some it takes just that. Unfortunately, Frank had to suffer before finding out he was bipolar. Maybe this was God's way of saying, "You need to be more humble, recognize your weaknesses, and give credit to others." Frank had taken many people for granted. He was not invincible, and he almost lost everything. I do not think he truly realized how fortunate he was and all of his blessings until now. Fortunately, he discovered this before it was too late. For some, they are not so lucky.

Next, I had to ease my conscience about past sins and mistakes I had made. Along the way, I had performed actions contradictory to my religion and wanted to confess my sins to God, asking for his forgiveness. Apprehensive, it had been many, many years since I had been to confession. I made an appointment at church, which happened to be June 6. Remembering this date, I was reminded of my aunt. Twenty years ago, she died on this day, her loss still felt. I knew she was with me that day as I spoke to the priest, giving me confidence and supporting my words. Highlighting the moments of my life, I shared my story, both the good and the bad. I revealed my sins, which included my visits to the psychic. Understanding, the priest gave me my penance which I performed before the altar. For twenty minutes I repeated the words, "I have my trust in God." I would continue to pray and put my trust in God just like I had done for so long. I also was resolved to confess my sins more frequently. I left with a clean heart and renewed spirit.

My trip to Myrtle Beach this year was much different. I was able to share a week with my family, something that never gets old, but this time I was more at ease. Sadly, before we left, I had to take Frank back to prison. In the past, I worried about returning home, not knowing what I would find. This time, I knew my husband was safe and sober.

Seeing Frank, I knew these past two weeks for him were difficult. However, this time he was better prepared and knew what to expect. I wouldn't call any time in prison easy, but at least he was being treated properly both medically and emotionally. His family was home waiting for him, and his job was still secure. He had made mistakes but needed to move forward. While he might regret his choices, he was not able to change them. Living in the past was something I did not want to do.

This would be Frank's last trip to jail. While sad, I was eager to end this chapter in our lives and the sooner he went, the quicker he would be home. As long as he continued to take his medicine, he should have the mindset to remain sober and never face this predicament again. Grateful for his doctor's intuition and the proper diagnosis, Frank could live his life like God meant him to. With so many blessings, it was a shame that he was unable to truly enjoy all that he had. Now, he saw life more clearly, sharing in the simple pleasures without having to rely on the numbing effects of alcohol.

I am content and satisfied with the choices I made and proud that we were able to overcome some of life's obstacles together. Steadfast in my faith, I had God's divine power to see me through. Life may have other hardships along the way, but I am convinced that if I remain a faithful person, I will have the strength to endure. I do not know what else is ahead for me or my family, but I welcome each day with a positive attitude hoping for a bright future. Take it from me, life may not play out exactly like you wish, but there is a purpose for all of us and a reason we are asked to take on a particular role. With patience and persistence, we can all have a happy ending.

MARYANNE

The first time I spoke of the possibility that my dad was an alcoholic was when I was in the sixth grade. "My dad is an alcoholic," my friend Jessica told me. "My mom says my dad is, but I don't think so," I replied.

Growing up, I didn't believe that my father had any problems. I loved him with all my heart, and I didn't understand why my mother was always getting mad at him. I remember they would argue, and I always sided with my father. I remember him coming home from business trips, and I was always so excited to see him. He'd have souvenirs for me from whatever city he was in, and I'd accept them all with a big smile and open arms. I even remember when he finally moved back home from having his own apartment; I was crying because I was so happy he was finally home. Then I got older.

I realized that my family wasn't like most other families when I was about middle school age. I was self-conscious of my friends coming over because I didn't want them to hear the screaming and shouting that erupted from my parents. Whenever this happened, I'd shut my door and try to make a lot of noise to cover up their yelling. I especially didn't want to introduce them to a father who was asleep on the couch in the middle of the afternoon. Whenever a new friend would come over, I just marked up my dad's sleeping to him being exhausted from a business trip. I recall my parents even arguing because my cousin, who my mother babysat during the summer, didn't want to come over anymore because my parents fought so much. Instead of realizing that the source of the arguments was my father's addiction, I was mad at her.

The first major realization I had of my father's addictions was when my mom packed up my younger sisters in the car and we drove to my dad's office. He hadn't been answering his phone all afternoon, so when we pulled up to the office park and his car was still there, we immediately knew something was wrong. My mom ran into his office, and there he was, passed out on his desk. There he was, my father, my hero—cherry-faced and incoherent. My mother never shielded my sisters and me from his behavior and problems, and actually often spoke to us about it. I saw and heard a lot of things that were very adult for a child. I think that is what has made me more mature than most of my peers and also maternal toward my sisters. At times, I even find myself lecturing my own mother.

I sometimes wonder how I am the person I am. Maybe it's because I spent so much time with my grandparents when I was growing up. I feel like I have a strong set of morals and values that weren't necessarily imposed on me by my parents. Maybe they came from growing up in the church, which my mom made me go to every Sunday. I always hated going, but looking back now, it is the foundation of my faith today. I lost faith in God when I was in my teens because I couldn't understand how He could let so many horrible things happen to my family. As I grew up and continue to grow, I realize how He was and is always there for us and helping my father. My mother has taught me a lot about faith, and because her belief is so strong, it has helped me to rebuild mine. Too many crazy situations have occurred that can only be explained as divine intervention. I know as God continues to show himself in mysterious ways to me throughout my life and continues to bless me with so many wonderful gifts, my faith and love in Him has grown and will continue to grow as I get older.

Growing up and seeing my parents made me not want to be like them as I grew older. In high school and the early part of my college years, I never drank alcohol. I had friends who did, but I swore to myself that was something I never wanted to try. It had caused everyone I loved so much pain and hurt that I couldn't possibly understand why anyone would want to. I soon began to realize that not everyone who drinks is an alcoholic, and you don't have to drink to get drunk. This was something that I could never understand growing up.

I've always loved my dad because he is *my* dad. He's the one that God gave to me. I have fond memories of him from when I was younger. He would sometimes come upstairs and tell me stories to help me fall asleep. If I fell asleep before he made it up to see me, he'd put a loose rubber band around my wrist so that way I knew he came and checked. I remember watching Saturday morning cartoons with him every weekend and resting my head on his stomach, hearing the comforting sounds of his heartbeat while we ate cereal or, if I was lucky, Coke floats.

I also have horrible memories of his addiction. Sadly, I recall many more of these than of the happy times. Once we were at the beach with my family when I was very young, probably about six, and my dad had snuck away and drank straight from a bottle out of my grandfather's liquor cabinet. He noticed that I saw him and held up a finger to his lips to let me know not to tell anyone. Even being so young, I had a feeling that what he was doing was wrong.

On "Take your Daughter to Work Day," he left me at the office with my uncles and grandfather while he had to run "errands" by himself. When he came back, I knew immediately where he had gone. It has become a sixth sense for me. I can tell from the corner of my eye if my dad has been drinking or not. It's in his posture, speech, and even his eyes. My mom would sometimes try to play it off as him being tired or from the stresses of work, but I was always knew what it really was. He came back from his "errands," and he was not the same man who had left forty-five minutes prior. He was acting so strangely, and his speech was different. He couldn't focus. He kept trying to pick a fight with my grandfather, and I couldn't understand why, or why would you soberly do that in front of your child. He was threatening to not go to my grandparents' for Christmas Eve, a family tradition, which immediately made me start to cry. When we finally left from the workday, on the way back home he kept offering to let me take the wheel. I was only twelve, and normally this may be exciting for any kid of that age, but to me, knowing what kind of state my father was in, I was terrified. How was I, an inexperienced driver, a preteen, going to get us home with a drunk driver? Thank God that He let us get home safely.

My parents would always involve my sisters and me in their fights. I remember on countless occasions coming home from school to find out my parents were considering getting a divorce. That or being told that we were going to have to move because my dad was going to lose his job because he was passed out again. I remember my mom confiding in me that she was scared we were going to lose our beautiful home and have to move into an apartment. When I was in high school, my mom would often talk about how she would not be able to afford to pay for my college and I would need to start working more hours to help pay for the family. Not until I was much older, at least eighteen, did I come to the realization that this was all talk. That being said, I grew up in a very unstable household. I remember so many times waking up at three in the morning because my mother would be sleeping in the other room with my sister, and my dad would rip open their bedroom door and wake the whole house up to pick a fight with my mother.

They would scream at the top of their lungs, and I would silently cry in my room. I just wanted to go to sleep, but found it difficult as I worried about my family's future.

My father's addiction was always bad, but it became worse when I entered high school and college. While in high school, I vividly remember a fight between my parents. This particular battle ended with a taxi cab arriving at my house and taking my father to a friend's. That night my dad had come home drunk and my mother confronted him with strip club receipts and bar tabs. He was supposed to have taken a client out earlier that day for lunch, but she found receipts of a different nature. He vehemently denied them, as he always did, and then the yelling escalated to screaming. That was the night that I found out my father had cheated on my mom when I was very young. He also started packing his bag because he said he was moving out because he "couldn't take it anymore." I immediately started bawling. This happened a lot—my father threatening to move—but it didn't change the amount of tears. I begged him to please not go, but he didn't listen. When the taxi came to pick him up and he got in, I hated my father.

One weekend, I had come back from college to visit my family. My dad hadn't come home, but my mother and I had a good idea of where to find him. We always knew to look over at the local sports bar, because that's where we'd usually find his car. Needless to say, there was his car, parked right in front of the restaurant. My mom and I decided to go in and sit down and just watch him. There he was, perched on his stool next to all the other local alcoholics. They all knew each other by name, and if you listened to them talk, it didn't make any sense. It broke my heart that they all seemed to know each other so well. Once my mother and I had had enough, we stood up and asked him to leave with us. He refused so we left with his keys and prayed he'd make it home safe.

On a different occasion when we couldn't find Dad, I had gone on my own to see if he was at the bar. He had finally figured out that we knew where he was going, so he started parking behind the building. When I drove behind the building, I saw his Infiniti and decided to face my father myself. I remember walking into the restaurant, straight up to the bar, and tapping his shoulder. He turned around, looked at me, and with his red face, very sternly said, "*Leave!*" I refused and said, "No, Dad. Please come home with me," and all he said, in his drunk state was, "*Leave!*" I started crying in the middle of the sports bar. I pulled his hand and made a fool of myself to get him to leave with me, but he wouldn't. I finally managed to get him outside into the parking lot, but he wouldn't budge and refused to get in the car. My mother finally showed up, and we somehow got him home. I think it was the threats of calling 9–1-1 that convinced him to leave.

Once I realized that my dad's actions were a result of his addiction, I started to learn to forgive him. Instead of being so angry to see him in his intoxicated state, I started to feel bad for him. Granted, I was still very upset, but I had to realize that this was a disease and not my father. Believe me that this is incredibly hard to do, especially when you come back from your family's beach vacation to find your house destroyed, your pets' food bowls empty, and your father looking and smelling as if he hasn't showered in a week. There were the times spent pleading, in the middle of the neighborhood, to get out of the car, because my dad was drunk and shouldn't be driving. Luckily we have kind, caring neighbors, who helped to balance him up the street back to our house.

I always tried to pretend that his drinking didn't affect me, and that it was his problem and I was going to live my life without the burdens of his addiction. When I was away at college, it was easier to ignore the problems at home. My mom and sisters would call me to talk to me about my dad, and I was always sympathetic but so glad to not be home. I'll never forget the day I had to stop ignoring the problems at home. One of my psychology courses was about to start, and I got a phone call from my mother. I figured it would be quick, so I answered. She sounded panicked, and I told her if it was bad news to not tell me until later. Of course being her, she couldn't help herself and she told me she saw my dad almost flip his car in front of the local high school, and he was taken away by the police. I was mortified. I started crying on the spot and ran to the nearest bathroom. I knew everyone in my class was wondering what had happened, but I wasn't about to divulge my family's biggest secret.

I'm a very private person, and not until recently have I even told my closest of friends about my father's addiction. I know it shouldn't be embarrassing for me because it's my father's problem; however, I don't want them to see my dad in a negative light because *he is* my father. I feel he's an extension of me, and I don't want him to only be known as an alcoholic. My father was always the life of the party, the guy everyone wanted to be around because he made them laugh. He was always incredibly generous to the people he cared about, and even acquaintances. He's a good man, and that's how I want people to know him, not as a belligerent alcoholic.

Once my father hit rock bottom and started cleaning up his life, things got a little easier. Immediately there was much less fighting in our house, and everyone seems a lot happier. I wish I could say that I don't worry if my dad is drunk when I come home from work or that I'm not suspicious when I look at him from the corner of my eye, but growing up constantly being on watch, I can't help it. Alcoholism put a major strain on our relationship, but it doesn't change the fact that I'm still his daughter and he'll always be my father. Now that he has been diagnosed with bipolarity, it helps to explain many of his behaviors. However, the strong medication he is on makes him not the father that I remember. He's a very distant, quieter, and calmer version of his former self, but I prefer this man to the explosive, dangerous one he was before.

Now our house is a lot quieter. We're still dealing with our memories of the past and working on our relationships. It's weird having to learn to function without a raging alcoholic living under the same roof. The alcoholic is still here; he's just sober. We still never have sat down and talked about everything that has happened. My dad has apologized many times, but only with words. He's never explained his behavior to me and my sisters or listened to how we felt about the disease and what kind of affect it's had on us. I believe we can work on having a happy family in the future. I know my father is frustrated because my sisters and I always go to our mother for advice and just to talk to about our lives. My mother was always the caregiver and always was there for us. She was there for every sporting event, made sure we always had a cake on our birthdays, and made sure we were always ready for school the next day. My dad tried, but work and alcohol kept him pretty occupied. I'm excited to start to get to know my father, as his sober self, and see who the man is behind the mask of alcohol. I hope that one day in the future, I'll feel comfortable enough to sit down and talk with him as a friend, and as a father that I always wished for.

MINDY

"Daddy's little girl" is a phrase I never understood, or what a girl did to be able to become one. Growing up as a child, I cannot say I had a relationship with my father. I only knew him as the one who provided the roof over my head, who controlled what I did, and who had top authority in the household. I have dealt with an alcoholic father since I was little and never really understood the true meaning until I matured and was in high school. My family and I could never rely on my father, and it was so hard to have to base everything around my father. One slip with my dad and our lives could change forever.

As a child, I remember the times my parents would always fight. However, I never knew what they were fighting about. My father would sometimes act out in physical ways, but most of the time, it was just verbal toward my mom. One tiny thing would set my dad off. I remember on the weekends, when I had nothing going on, my friends would call me asking to play. I would think my parents would say yes because there was no reason I should have not been able to. I would go to my mom first, hoping she would say yes, but instead she tossed out the phrase, "Go ask your father." So I would ask my dad, as he was laying back in his recliner, if I could go hang out with my friends. He would say no. After begging and begging, he would still say no and have no reasoning. Some children would say that happens to them all the time, but this happened many times when my mom would always be on my side. My father just wanted the control on us. I just remember, when I could hang out, I wanted to go to other people's houses because the fighting between my parents was always an embarrassment. Sometimes I would just stay outside and play with my friends if we were at my place. Of course, we had an African Gray Bird who loved repeating things said and screaming the way my parents did. I never understood why my father acted this way, and I never knew what alcohol could do to a person.

During middle school, I feel like I finally realized what was going on. I knew my dad had a drinking problem. My mother would now take her anger at my father out on us. I would hope to come home to a sober father, but I knew on a weekend that was never going to happen. I remember my sisters, my mom, and I would sometimes have to question if he was drunk or not. Soon enough, even the majority of the weekdays consisted of my father being drunk. My father was almost always drunk. I hated knowing I could lose my father at any moment and my life could change in a split second. I could never imagine children at this age having to deal with this situation, but my sisters and I had to. I believe this will make us stronger.

High school was a different story. I finally realized the cause of my dad's anger and weird actions. Freshman year was when I had enough. I would go off on my dad when he was drunk, thinking I could talk some sense in him. That would never happen. I just caused my dad to be even angrier and cause hate toward him more. I almost wanted him to be passed out on the recliner on Friday just so I did not have to ask if I could go out or even deal with him. However, his health would still cross my mind even when I was gone. I felt so bad for my mom having to sit at home dealing with him all alone. But I knew she wanted us to be happy, and our happiness was out of the house, away with our friends. I remember my father always giving us what we wanted. One year we all received laptops for no reason, or we all got manicure and pedicures. When I first got my license, he used to let me go pick up food he wanted or his slushy he always got from BP. He would pay for my friends and me to get something and even put gas in my car. I felt he was always dishing out money to me. Usually, we would receive those kinds of things on special occasions. I almost felt my dad was trying to buy our love, because that was the only way he knew to make us happy. My dad loved going to Dairy Queen and other fast food restaurants randomly, but when we knew he left to go there, he was also going to pick up a bottle too. I hated coming home knowing my dad was still drunk. My father could not even let us enjoy our vacations away from him. He could not even take care of our pets when he would stay at home. He was like a child who needed a babysitter. My mother would just be on edge the whole time at the beach and worrying about how my dad would sound on the phone when she would call. I felt bad she could not even enjoy herself at the beach with her whole family. I wanted her to tell us what was going on because I knew when she was not okay, but I also hated hearing my mom throw out the negatives and what could happen to us all the time.

Later on in high school, I just wanted my dad to receive help. He was going deeper and deeper into this horrible situation, and I knew he needed to hit rock bottom before he could go up. I hated seeing my father passed out on the floor or falling down the steps. I hated my mom having to call the cops because he was so incoherent and wanted to drive. I hated watching my dad literally run from the cops and hop over our six foot fence just because he could not think straight. I hated knowing the strongest person in our family could not even stand up most of the time. I did not have a father. He was almost nothing to me but a provider. I had an older boyfriend who I almost feel took the place of him. He took care of me, paid for me, did everything in his power to make me happy, and provided that comfort from a male figure I did not have.

My father finally had to face jail time and went to rehab. He is now sober and was diagnosed with bipolar disorder. My father and I still do not have the relationship I would like to have with my dad, but we are still working on it. I am just so proud of the outcome and how strong he is to still be alive and happy. He is the most fortunate person I know, with a loving family to support him and a job that understood his situation. I could never be as strong as my mother who stood by his side through thick and thin. That is the definition of a marriage. My parents have inspired me to be strong when in a marriage and know that God will make sure everything will be okay. If my parents can overcome this kind of struggle and be together, I think I can overcome any situation I have with my future husband. I can honestly say how proud I am of my mom. She is one of the strongest people I know, and I look up to her. I hope I will be as great of a wife as her one day.

MARISSA

You know the families who have the perfect house, with the white picket fence, loving siblings, and caring parents living inside? Well, my family is quite the opposite. Despite my father's disease, he has always been a great provider. But when it came to a father-daughter relationship, we never had anything close to one. Seeing my friends with a close relationship with their dads always made me jealous and wonder why my dad had to be an alcoholic and not spend anytime with me, unlike my friends. I never fully understood why we couldn't have a close relationship like other families.

When I was a little girl, I played sports such as softball, basketball, gymnastics, and other things. Unfortunately, I grew up with him never being there to cheer me on. Watching movies and seeing fathers cheering their kids on and supporting them in what they wanted to do made me wonder why I was different. My mom always went to my games or competitions alone, without my dad by her side. On the few occasions he managed to show up, he would be there either late or drunk. This made me embarrassed to have him around at any public event. It got to the point where I didn't even want him there. This also made it hard for me to invite my friends over. I was scared that he would be screaming or passed out drunk, sleeping on the couch once my friends arrived. As I got older, my friends and I would just joke about him bumping into the wall. But deep down, it honestly hurt seeing my father act this way. I never understood the disease and why my dad had to be held as a prisoner.

Being the youngest of three sisters, it would seem that we would we be close and talk to each other, comforting one another through the depressing times we went through. We did the total opposite and kept our feelings to ourselves. I look back on it now and wonder why we didn't talk things out. Thinking about the past, I believe if I talked with my sisters we could have a closer bond than we have now. Keeping it locked inside really didn't do us any good. Whenever my parents would be fighting, I would sit in my room and just listen. This wasn't really the best way to grow up, in fear. Staying strong was what my mom did for us. If she left my father, then we wouldn't have had money to survive and have a good life. She stuck through the hard days and kept our family together. She knew what was right for my sisters and me. If my sisters and I had only talked about our feelings together, it would have made us stronger. We could have helped each other through the torturous years, as opposed to hiding out in a desperate attempt to stay away from home as long as possible.

Still to this day, I have fears of my dad falling off the sober wagon and picking up that bottle again. If he did that, our lives would drastically change. He could lose his job as well as the house and go to jail for quite a long time. Knowing that now really makes me scared for my family's future. Our lives could change so quickly if he failed. When I was little, I did not really worry about these things happening. I wasn't old enough to understand what my dad was truly doing to himself and to the family. Now that I am at an age where I know what he was doing really makes me feel bad for my oldest sister. As a child, it was difficult to comprehend all that was happening. But since my sister was so much older than me and understood everything so clearly, I don't understand how she went through everything. I constantly saw my mother in pain, and I knew my father was the cause. It must have been completely different for my sister, being at the more mature age. Despite the gap in our personal relationship, we individually learned to get through this roller coaster.

Vacations are typically fun and exciting. Having my dad there was anything but that. We never really went anywhere together as I grew up, but when we did, it was not how spending a vacation together with that family should have been. When we went to Myrtle Beach visiting my father's side of the family, he would go off and drink, even if he knew he shouldn't. My parents would always fight and argue. Also, going on trips without my dad wasn't any better. When we left him alone in the house, it was as if we left a little kid there. This was scary to think about, because sometimes we would be gone for a week. It would make my mom stressed out to the point where she could not enjoy herself. She constantly worried about my dad not taking care of the pets or the house. Coming home from trips was tragic as well. The house looked as if it had been hit by a tornado! Everything was trashed, out of place, or simply gross. Our animals' food was filled with bugs! My mother quickly learned that vacations without my dad were not a good idea. It was hard seeing my mother go through all this pain that my father had brought upon her.

Since my father had this disease ever since I was a little girl, I barely have any good memories with him. We never did father-daughter days or events. The only slight memory I had with him was if he invited me to go to Dairy Queen with him to get some ice cream. The reason for him to ask me was because my mother did not trust him to go alone, knowing he would end up stopping at the nearest liquor store on the way home. But being the manipulative person he was, he would park on the side of a building and tell me he was going to be back real fast and to keep the doors locked.

Being as little as I was, I thought nothing of this. He got his booze even when I went with him. I would see my mother and father fight as well. I've seen them fight all the way to the basement over the bottle; it was like a scary movie that you could not take your eyes off of. I was too afraid to not watch, fearing my father would hurt her. Not having many loving memories with my father as a child really makes it hard to respect him as the person who he is today.

My mother was always there. She was the perfect loving mother who would do anything for her children. Not having the support of her husband behind her, she did whatever she could to make my sisters and me as happy as we could possibly be. She even taught CCD class, which was a religion class children took to get to know more about their faith. She sacrificed the little time she had for herself in the day to teach my sister's class for many years and also mine as well. She always puts others' wants and needs before her own at every given moment. I look up to my mother every day. I noticed as I grew up that my mom was such a strong person and realize that those years must have been torturous. My mom is in most of my childhood memories. We would sit in her room watching soap operas while just simply talking about our day. I was a momma's girl and always wanted to be around her. Still to this day, I talk to my mom about most things. I know she'll stand up for me and will be behind my every decision in life. Even if I do wrong, she will still support me and love me for whom I am. I have so much respect for my mom, I might not show it as much as I should, but she went through so much just for her girls. I love my mom with all my heart; she put out her all just to make our life the best it could be. She is my hero.

I still love my dad and respect everything he has done for the family, and I know all the suffering he brought to us was not in his hands. He was going through the same amount of torture as he had put upon us. I don't blame my father for what he has done in the past. All we can do is move forward. We still have a rocky relationship to this day. Even though he has been sober for the past two years, I never really sit down and actually talk to him. Whenever we are together, we sit in silence and we don't speak much to each other. I would love to one day just spend some time with my father and get to know him for who he actually is. Unfortunately, he's not going to be here forever. For now, he might physically be there, but spiritually I feel as if there is no one present when I'm around. I know he can open up with his co-workers, as well as my mother and his best friend. I have rarely seen that side of him as much as I truly would like to. I would love if one day my father and I could have a tight bond together between each other just like how my mom and I share. He will always be my dad, and through all the drama he caused for the family, I wouldn't want any other father other than him. One day, I would love to just spend time together as a family. Some people walk in and out of your lives, but family will always be there for you through thick and thin. I love my family and wouldn't change them for the world. I'd love to just go off on a family trip and get to know each other for who we truly are. Every one of them means everything to me, and I love them more than anything. Hopefully the day will come when we can all share a tight bond between each other after all the drama has been set aside. Through highs and lows, we will always be there for each other, no matter what.